Berlitz

EGYPT

- A ✓ in the text denotes a highly recommended sight

- A complete A–Z of practical information starts on p. 115

- Extensive mapping throughout: on cover flaps and in text

Although we make every effort to ensure the accuracy of the information in this guide, changes do occur. If you have any new information, suggestions or corrections to contribute, we would like to hear from you. Please write to Berlitz Publishing at one of the above addresses.

Text:	Jack Altman
Editor:	Sarah Hudson, Donald Greig
Photography:	Pete Bennett (p. 61 Julian Parish)
Layout:	Suzanna Boyle
Cartography:	🦅 Falk-Verlag, Hamburg
Thanks to:	Amin Atwa, Nahed Rizk and colleagues at the Egyptian Tourism Authority, and Mohammed Salem Ragaa Younes and colleagues at Misr Travel for their invaluable help in the preparation of this guide.
Cover photograph:	the Sphinx and Pyramids at Gîza

CONTENTS

Egypt and the Egyptians

In the middle of the desert, eastern terminus of the vast Sahara, Egypt has her own eternal miracle, which cuts defiantly through the burning, arid wilderness to the Mediterranean – the Nile. Rising in the remotest African uplands, the Nile has long swept fertilizing silts down into its valley, giving rise 5,000 years ago to one of the greatest civilizations known to man. The Nile is Egypt's life-blood.

To understand the importance of the mighty river for Egyptians, stand on its western bank at Aswân, where, the desert is so close that you can pick up a handful of sand and throw it in the water. At the southern end of town, the dam harnesses the river's power in the perennial struggle to nourish the country's teeming millions. For nearly 1,000km (625 miles) – from Abu Simbel to Cairo – narrow fields full of irrigated crops line the banks. A cloudless sky adds its blessing, with the hot sun nurturing at least two harvests a year. The early Egyptians saw divinity in the sun, the great partner of their river, and they named it Ra, and raised great temples in its honour.

Although the influence of the classical Greeks seems to have been lost in the melting pot of successive invasions, that of the ancient Egyptians has been retained, at least insomuch as their descendants still till the fields, work in the factories and sell their wares in the *souks*. Those claiming to be the most direct heirs are the Copts, who embraced the faith preached by Saint Mark, founder of one of the oldest churches in Christendom. Copts still play a significant role in Egyptian life, and Coptic churches are found in almost every town. Boutros Ghali, Secretary General of the United Nations, is their most prominent son.

Even among the Moslem majority, however, the ancient Egyptian lineage is physically apparent. As depicted in temple friezes and sculptures, the proud profiles of pharaohs and 5

Y*ou'll find public water fountains everywhere, but if you're thirsty, mineral water is safer.*

while much later, both Mamelukes and Turks arrived, bringing with them the richness of their customs and cuisine.

Egypt has always held an irresistible fascination for the traveller. Pyramids and palms, the Nile, the Sphinx and the desert – all these are enough to make anyone dream of at least one visit, not to mention the added attraction of beach resorts along the Red Sea and Mediterranean coasts.

To find Egypt's true glory, however, just scratch the surface of a pyramid. Ancient civilizations continue to exert a limitless magnetism on art historians, archaeologists, theologians, philosophers, charlatans and mystics – although this deeply rooted sense of history actually gets to us all.

Visit the four mighty stone figures of Ramses II's monument in Abu Simbel, and you might begin to share the ancient Egyptians' feeling for the divinity of the pharaohs. Walk through the sacred temples of Luxor and Karnak, or Thebes' eerie 'city of the dead', and you will realize how serious

princesses, artisans and warriors, can still be seen in the streets of Cairo, Aswân and Luxor. Others bear the traits of numerous invaders. Between 1100 and 332 BC came Libyans, Persians and black Africans from Nubia. Around the 7th century, Arabs imported **6** their language and religion,

the ancient Egyptians were about their religion.

Wherever you may travel in Egypt, you will encounter the places and names of a rich and colourful history: Alexandria, Antony and Cleopatra, Tutankhamun, Memphis, Sinai, El-Alamein and Suez. The key to modern Egypt, however – as well as guardian of its past – remains Cairo.

Compared to the eternal life of the river, Cairo is a 'new' city – only 1,000 years old. In the shadow of Gîza's pyramids, the Cairenes have raised countless monuments to the glory of Islam, making their city a centre of Arabic civilization. Moslems throughout the world still regard Cairo as the treasure-house of Islamic art, architecture and learning.

As capital of the most populous nation in the Arab world, Cairo faces urgent problems. In recent years, the population

*P*alm trees and farmland mark the fertile Fayyoum Oasis in the middle of the desert.

*A*ncient and modern: a panorama of Cairo in sandstone, from the battlements of Saladin's Citadel, built in 1207.

has shot up at a rate of nearly 4,000 a day; the earthquake on 12 October 1992, which devastated the oldest neighbourhoods, added to the problem. Many are forced to make their homes in the tombs of medieval cemeteries on the east end of the city, while swarms of pedestrians, cars and overloaded buses fight for possession of the city's streets, all stirring up the blanket of fine **8** desert dust that infrequent and brief rains cannot wash away. Cairo is arguably the loudest city in the world.

The long-suffering Cairenes, however, face their difficulties with both hope and a smile. The government is continually coming up with momentous projects designed to catapult the country into the future, and even if the plans do get bogged down in skeins of red tape, one of them is bound to work some day.

A Brief History

In the fertile Nile Valley, Stone Age Egyptians happily turned from hunting to the steadier existence of farming. By 8000 BC, they were rearing cattle and growing wheat and barley imported from neighbouring Asia. In exchange, handsome stoneware, ceramics and jewellery were exported. From Mesopotamia's script, they developed their own hieroglyphic writing, and on papyrus made by pounding strips of Nile reeds together, the written history of ancient Egypt began to unfold.

Old and Middle Kingdoms

Upper and Lower Egypt were united by King Menes (1st Dynasty, 3000 BC), who was the first to wear the 'double crown' so often seen in pharaonic art. Memphis, a short distance south of Cairo, was the capital. Unity brought with it wealth, power and progress, and some three centuries later the Old Kingdom (2780-2250 BC), headed by King Djoser of the 3rd Dynasty, was established. He built the step pyramid at Saqqara (see p.40), thus inaugurating the epoch of the great pyramids.

Within 200 years, mathematics and the organization of manpower had advanced so far that Cheops and his son, Chephren, were in a position to construct the colossal pyramids and Sphinx at Gîza (see p.38). Seeking to consolidate this astounding human achievement with the halo of divinity, the pharaohs of the 5th Dynasty (2440-2315 BC) proclaimed themselves to be sons of the great sun god, Ra. Soon provincial lords challenged the royal authority, and the Old Kingdom was ended by civil war around 2250 BC.

The Middle Kingdom lasted for over four centuries (2000-1570 BC), during which time Egypt re-established itself as a rich and strong nation. The pharaohs stood at the top of a feudal order, and powerful nobles controlled each of the kingdom's *nomes* (provinces).

Supported by his vassals, the king marched from Thebes (Luxor), the new capital, south to Nubia and east into Palestine, conquering all in his path. Such adventures were afforded due to the wealth brought by major advances in irrigation, notably in the desert province of Fayyoum (see p.47).

As the conquerors' fortunes grew, their lands became more desirable to Egypt's warlike neighbours. One enemy people, the Hyksos, had a secret weapon to overcome even the bravest Egyptian foot soldier: the horse chariot. In the 17th century BC, rolling swiftly across Sinai and into the fertile delta, they forced the pharaohs retreat to Thebes (Luxor). The Hyksos chiselled triumphant signs in the form of horses and chariots – still visible today – on tomb and temple walls.

For a century, the Hyksos ruled Lower Egypt, but their power, although dominant in terms of chariots, stopped at the southern edge of the easily crossed delta. There the desert began and the infantry of Upper Egypt came into their own.

New Kingdom

Following the expulsion of the Hyksos in 1570 BC, the pharaohs began to consider exactly how the country was run, and implemented a number of reforms. First, they succeeded in prising power away from the feudal nobles and concentrating it amongst themselves, and then they improved their military capacity by building chariots. Egypt soon developed into a well-organized and disciplined imperial state, headed by a monarch who was intent on both foreign conquests and personal glory.

During the New Kingdom (1570-1100 BC), ancient Egypt reached the dazzling pinnacle of its splendour, with the construction of the massive temples and tombs at Luxor (see p.50), Karnak (see p.56) and Abu Simbel (see p.89), and the return of Egyptian armies from Syria and deepest Africa with rich booty and hundreds of slaves. The wealth of the country was unrivalled, and much of it went to glorify the god-kings who ruled it.

Some of Egypt's greatest rulers were those of the 18th Dynasty. The three pharaohs named Thutmosis vastly extended the empire's borders. Hatshepsut, wife of Thutmosis II and stepmother of Thutmosis III, reigned for a period as Queen of Egypt, and built a magnificent funerary temple at Deir el-Bahari (see p.63).

Amenophis III (1417-1379 BC) ruled New Kingdom Egypt at its zenith. Much of the Great Temple of Amon at Karnak (see p.56) is his work. His son, Amenophis IV, favoured mystical meditation and decreed a new religion, displacing the age-old pantheon of Egyptian gods by the One True God, Aton. He changed his name to Akhenaton ('He Who Pleases Aton'), and with Queen Nefertiti moved his capital to what is now Tell El-Amarna in Middle Egypt. He made bitter enemies of the powerful priests of Amon at Thebes, however, and his death left the country in disarray.

His young son-in-law Tutankhaton (1361-1351 BC) – who later changed his name to Tutankhamun – reigned too briefly to restore order – but long enough to amass the only pharaonic treasure to escape the tomb-plunderers more or less intact (see p.81).

*E*ntrance to the unique temple of Kom Ombo, shared by both crocodile and falcon gods.

11

Last of the great pharaohs – Ramses III spent much of his time fighting invaders.

The 18th Dynasty ended as power was usurped by an energetic and able soldier, founder of the 19th Dynasty, Ramses I. His successor, Seti, won back all of Egypt's foreign possessions by renewed conquests. Then came Ramses II. This pharaoh had trouble maintaining the empire, but also became the greatest and most prolific builder Egypt had ever known. His long reign (1304-1237 BC) saw the huge temple rise at Abu Simbel (see p.89), and the great hypostyle hall finished at Karnak (see p.56), plus the completion of countless other huge monuments, many of them honoured with colossal statues in his own image. With a firm hand, Ramses II quietened the Semitic tribes which had been causing disorder in his eastern provinces. One tribe, the Israelites, he kept under strict control for years, building temples in the delta before allowing them to leave Egypt and return to the land of their forefathers.

Pharaohs of the 20th Dynasty preserved Egypt's greatness until 1100 BC, after which later dynasties never regained the glory. Foreign invasions became frequent and the Persians ousted the last native Egyptian pharaoh in the 4th century BC. The country then passed into Greek hands, when it was conquered – practically without resistance – by Alexander the Great in 332 BC.

Under Greece and Rome

After Alexander's death in 323 BC, his Hellenistic empire was up for grabs among his generals. In 305 BC, in a country divided between two cultures – with Hellenistic dominating Egyptian – Ptolemy, governor of Egypt, assumed the title of pharaoh. Alexandria, the conqueror's city which had been founded on the Mediterranean shore (see p.42), was the most civilized and significant centre in the Hellenistic world; but the power of knowledge and learning, symbolized by the great library which was Alexandria's glory, could do little against the legions of Rome.

For 20 years (51-30 BC), Queen Cleopatra VII used wit and charm – first on Caesar, and then on the Roman general Mark Antony – to keep her country free. She had no

---

Cleopatra

Many Ptolemaic princesses were named Cleopatra, but it was Cleopatra VII (69-30 BC) who left her mark on history. Married to her younger brother, Ptolemy XII, when she was 17 years old, she later overthrew him with Caesar's help. She followed the conqueror to Rome, deserted her second husband and eventually bore a son, whom she named Caesarion. (It has never been established without doubt that the father was Julius Caesar, but it suited everyone to believe it at the time.) For a while, Caesarion reigned alongside his mother as Ptolemy XIV.

Some time after Caesar's murder, Mark Antony turned up in Egypt and fell quickly under Cleopatra's spell. They were married in 36 BC. At the end of her reign, after the crushing naval defeat at Actium, Cleopatra had a servant bring a basket of figs containing a serpent; its bite put an end to her torment.

Despite the charm she held for Julius Caesar and Mark Antony, it is recorded that Cleopatra was neither strikingly beautiful nor popular. The Romans feared or despised her.

13

chance with Caesar's heir, Octavius (later Augustus). who was interested only in consolidating his Roman Empire. After Mark Antony's defeat at the naval battle of Actium (30 BC), Cleopatra committed suicide, and Hellenistic Egypt died with her. For centuries the land was reduced to provincial subservience, ruled first from Rome and later from Constantinople (Istanbul).

The Arab Empire

The wave of armies which poured forth from Arabia in the 7th century ranks as one of history's most baffling phenomena. Before the time of the Prophet Mohammed the Arabs constituted a few dozen Semitic tribes living in a hot and dusty land. Existing on little more than camel's milk and dates, they traded by means of camel caravan and carried out raids on their neighbours. With the arrival of Islam ('Submission to God's Will'), however, the Arabs started to achieve conquests which in time were to change the world.

In the city of Mecca, Mohammed was a merchant much given to meditation in a cool cave in the mountains. There, in AD 612, he heard a celestial voice, which commanded him to communicate the new faith. Over the next 20 years, up until his death in AD 632, Mohammed delivered the 114 *suras* (chapters) which make up the Koran, the beautiful text which has become the constitution and inspiration of the Moslem world.

In the early years of Islam, believers were organized as a small, close-knit society which was led by Mohammed himself. As the community then expanded, armies were formed and military operations begun. Within a swift century of Mohammed's death, Arab forces had conquered the Middle East including Persia, North Africa, and parts of Spain and France.

Invaded by the Arabs in AD 639, Egypt was among the first countries to fall. At the southern tip of the delta, the Arabs made their military camp, El-Fustat, the country's capital. Within 300 years, Egypt had become one of the Arab Empire's most important political, religious and military centres. Then, around AD 968, a powerful dynasty called the Fatimids swept in from the Maghreb to seize Egypt and replaced the old capital with Al-Qahira, the City of Victory – Cairo.

At the vigorous height of Fatimid rule, which lasted two centuries, Cairo enjoyed one of its richest cultural periods. The renowned El-Azhar University and Mosque (see p.24) date from these times, and still remain a spiritual beacon to all Islam, as well as a summit of Fatimid architecture.

The armies of Saladin overran the empire of the Fatimids in 1169. Saladin, famous for his campaigns against the Crusaders in Palestine and Syria, then established his own dynasty in Egypt – the Ayyubids. His descendants were subsequently ousted by a new wave of usurpers, who were mostly Turkish soldiers who had been slaves (*mameluke*) of the Ayyubids, and in a series of short and violent reigns, Mameluke strongmen succeeded one another from 1251 to 1517. Despite their unstable rule, Mameluke power started to spread through both Syria and Palestine. In Cairo, they built countless palaces and mosques of exquisite beauty.

Mameluke power was defeated – but not destroyed – when Egypt was conquered by the fast-moving and efficient armies of the Ottoman Turks in 1517. Three years later, Suleiman the Magnificent came to the throne in Constantinople (Istanbul), ushering in the Ottoman Empire's most brilliant and powerful era.

After Suleiman's death in 1566, however, his dominions fell into a decline that dragged on for some three and a half centuries. The Egyptian province lost the benefits of efficient government and internal order as provincial Mameluke lords clamoured for many of their old prerogatives from the Ottoman pasha in Cairo. Instability returned with Mameluke rule, and Egypt lurched haplessly and helplessly from crisis to crisis in a decadent and backward culture.

15

*S*ultan Qait Bey's fort stands on the site of Alexandria's famous lighthouse, one of the Seven Wonders of the Ancient World.

16

Napoleon and Mohammed Ali

Egypt's first contact with the modern world came in 1798 in the form of a French military expedition under the young Napoleon Bonaparte. His primary interest lay in blocking Britain's route across the Red Sea to India, but the expedition also included a group of scientists and archaeologists.

Although, for a time, Napoleon brought a certain order and discipline to Egypt's government, and laid the foundations for later archaeological expeditions, the French fleet was destroyed by the British in the Battle of Aboukir in 1798. Napoleon sneaked off to pursue his career in France, and over the next three years the remnants of the French force returned home. Egypt seemed ready to slip into torpor and anarchy once again.

Among the Ottoman troops who had arrived to counter the French invasion was a young officer from Albanian lineage called Mohammed Ali. With cunning and ruthless force, he succeeded in seizing power and having the sultan appoint him Pasha of Egypt. On 1 May 1811, he invited all his rivals (Mameluke notables) to a banquet in the Citadel in Cairo. As the 'guests' entered, the gates slammed shut and they were massacred by the new pasha's troops. Mameluke political power – an important factor in Egypt since 1251 – had reached its final bloody end.

Fascinated by the modern methods he had observed in Napoleon's army, Mohammed Ali proceeded to reform his own and to build a fleet on Western lines, using European advisors. Moves were made to modernize both commerce and agriculture, and recently irrigated lands were planted with cotton. The country started to generate great wealth, and although the people remained desperately poor, the ruler accumulated a fabulous fortune.

Between 1832 and 1841, Mohammed Ali twice waged war on his sovereign in Istanbul and almost succeeded in capturing the Ottoman capital. Forced to recognize the virtu- **17** ally independent power of his one-time vassal, the sultan decreed that the office of Pasha of Egypt should be hereditary in the house of Mohammed Ali. The title of pasha was then upgraded to *khedive*, viceroy in the Ottoman hierarchy.

Later rulers of the House of Mohammed Ali, however, did not live up to their ancestor's energy and vision. In 1869, the Suez Canal (started by Khedive Said Pasha in 1859) was opened to navigation during the rule of Khedive Ismail, who allowed his ambitious projects to be financed by unscrupulous bankers. When he was unable to repay the millions borrowed at usurious rates of interest, the European powers forced him to appoint British and French 'advisors' in his government. The British soon succeeded in gaining political and military control.

The 20th Century

During World War I, Egypt's strategic location was vital to the British, with Cairo as the staging-point for the Allied offensive to wrest Syria, Palestine and Arabia from Ottoman control. Even before the fall of the Ottoman Empire, Egypt's British governors declared the puppet *khedive's* independence from Turkish sovereignty. Although Prince Fuad then styled himself King of Egypt on his accession in 1917, real power remained in foreign hands.

Following the war, nationalist sentiment crystallized in the Wafd Party, under Saad Zaghloul. In the 1924 elections for a Chamber of Deputies, the anti-British Wafd won a large majority and remained the prime nationalist force for decades.

World War II spotlighted Egypt's strategic importance. In 1940, Italian forces pushed deep from Libya into Egypt, before being turned back by British Empire troops. In the following year, General Rommel's brilliant desert army recaptured the ground and rolled swiftly into Egypt. They were halted in 1942 at El-Alamein, under 100km (60 miles) from Alexandria (see p.45). As a turning-point for the Allies, this meant that by the end of

Historical Landmarks

BC	**Old Kingdom** 3000–2250	1st–6th Dynasties Saqqara, Gîza Pyramids
	Middle Kingdom 2000–1570	11th–12th Dynasties Hyksos chariot invasion
	New Kingdom 1570–1100	18th–20th Dynasties Tombs at Luxor, Abu Simbel
	Late Period 1100–332	21st–30th Dynasties Libyan, Nubian, Assyrian, Persian, Greek invasions:
	Ptolemaic Period 332–30	Rule of Ptolemies I–XIV and Cleopatra
	Roman-Byzantine Era 30 BC–AD 639	Saint Mark brings Christi- anity in AD 40
AD	**Arab Empire** 639–1251	Umayyad, Abbasid, Fatimid, Ayyubid dynasties
	Mamelukes 1251–1517	Cairo mosques/mausoleums
	Ottoman Rule 1517–1914 1811 1869	 Turkish rule from Istanbul Mohammed Ali dynasty Suez Canal opens
	Egyptian Monarchy 1917–1952	Under British control, King Farouk abdicates
	Republic period 1953–70 1972 1979 1981 1981	 Nasser becomes President Aswân High Dam completed Peace Treaty with Israel President Sadat assassinated Mubarak becomes President

the year, Egypt was again securely in British hands.

In 1936 King Farouk had come to the throne. Despite initial good intentions, Farouk soon succumbed to the pleasures of palace intrigue and luxurious living. Government suffered, and military defeat by Israel in 1948 was followed by diplomatic defeat when the king tried to claim full control over the Sudan and the Suez Canal. Unrest grew until he was overthrown in 1952 by a group of military officers led by General Mohammed Naguib. After a short time, Naguib was replaced by the mastermind behind the revolution, Colonel Gamal Abdel Nasser.

Nasser declared the country a Republic on 18 June 1953, and remained in power for 17 years. Despite his authoritarian rule, he excited the people with a passionate new pride and revitalized a sense of national identity. Under Egyptian government, the country rapidly emerged as a leader among Third World nations. Nasser began to overhaul and modernize the economy, making the symbol for this effort the Aswân High Dam. Its giant power stations generate huge quantities of electricity, meeting a third of Egypt's needs.

President Anwar Sadat succeeded Nasser in 1970 with less charismatic style, but his more moderate stance brought a stability desperately needed, for energy and resources had been continually under strain because of recurrent wars with Israel. After the humiliations of 1948, 1956 and 1967, partial success in 1973 restored Egyptian self-confidence and enabled Sadat to retrieve the Israeli-occupied Sinai in the historic peace treaty with Israel in 1979. Egypt's recognition of Israel, however, was fiercely opposed by other Arab leaders and was one of the reasons Sadat was assassinated by Moslem militants in 1981. The Arab League then acknowledged Egypt's significance to

Bougainvillea lends colour to a genteel neighbourhood in neocolonial Ismailiya.

the Arab world, reopening its headquarters in Cairo in 1990.

Although Hosni Mubarak's presidency has been less visionary than Nasser's, and less spectacular than Sadat's, his practical approach has earned him respect both at home and abroad. The problems are considerable. Unemployment is at 20 percent and child labour, though illegal, is common. A ponderous and often corrupt administration grapples with a burgeoning population, which is draining vital resources, a fact that was highlighted in 1992 in the chaotic aftermath of the most powerful earthquake Egypt has ever known. Overcrowding and illegal construction resulted in 600 dead – many of them children fleeing packed schools – and 10,000 injured.

Keenly aware of the crucial importance of both foreign investment and the tourist industry, however, Egyptians remain essentially moderate in their attitude to everyday life. Furthermore, they are able to draw strength from their proud and glorious past.

Where to Go

Cairo

The national capital marks the point at which Islam carried Egypt's story forward from the pharaohs, where the Nile Valley widens into the flat, fertile delta. It is the largest city in Africa (home to 13 million), and one of the most densely populated places on the planet, with an average of 75,000 people per square mile (or 29,000 per square kilometre). Here, by the side of the slow, silent-flowing Nile, a bewildering multitude of people live together in an intense bustle of activity.

The heart of the modern metropolis lies on the east bank of the Nile and extends on to the two islands of Gezira and Roda. Large, luxury hotels rise up on the river banks in this area, and Garden City's cooling greenery stretches along the waterfront. No fewer than four bridges span the waters between the landmark of Television Building to the north and the southern tip of Roda Island. One of the busiest, Tahrir Bridge (Kubry Al Tahrir/Kasr El Nil), crosses the main branch of the river from Gezira Island and enters the heart of the city, Tahrir Square.

Microcosm of Cairo's daily life, **Tahrir Square** (Midan Tahrir) throbs and rumbles all day long and half the night as well. The tremendous traffic roundabout is a rabbit warren of underground tunnels connecting pedestrian walkways and the metro system (built by the French and still being extended). In the square, pedlars and vendors take up time-honoured battle-stations each morning, waiting for the day's army of potential customers to hurry by. Here and there the occasional open space is filled with long queues of endlessly-patient Cairenes waiting for overstuffed buses – in which there is often no room – to arrive and depart.

Some of Cairo's most prestigious institutions surround Tahrir Square, including the renowned **Egyptian Museum** (see p.33), Ministry of Foreign

Affairs, American University, and the Nile Hilton, with its perfect people-watching café.

Leaving the square, Talaat Harb Street leads to the beginning of Cairo's chic shopping and business street, **Kasr El-Nil**. Cinemas, cafés, tea-shops and restaurants abound along these thoroughfares, providing refuge from the bustle of daytime commerce. At night the main streets are brightly lit and thronged with window-shoppers, strollers and young Cairenes on their way to the theatre or cinema. If it all becomes overpowering, try escaping to the delightful Nile-side promenade of Cairo's **El-Corniche**, which you'll find due west of any point in the city centre.

ISLAMIC CAIRO

Wherever you go in Cairo, the fantasy architecture of mosque domes and minarets rises up above the jumble of rooftops. The city preserves a rich tradition of Islamic artistry, and even the dark veneer of time cannot rob these imaginative structures of their charm. Go east from Tahrir Square, past the large, 19th-century Republic (Abdin) Palace to Ahmed Maher Square, and from there through a busy market area to reach the massive, cylindrical bastions of **Bab Zuweila**, an imposing gate set in the medieval city walls. Many a condemned criminal or opponent

Bab Zuweila gate is more cheerful now that they no longer hang people there.

of the ruler has been hanged from this gate in times past.

The two minarets on top of the gate actually belong to the adjoining **mosque**. This was finished in 1420 by the Mameluke Sultan El-Moayyad. Following a spell spent in Bab Zuweila's infamous prison, he vowed if he was ever freed he would build a mosque. Once released, he designed a particularly beautiful building with outstanding stonework and a pretty courtyard garden. Ask to see the *segn* (prison), and climb the stairway to the top of Bab Zuweila – there's a marvellous view.

Continuing north on Muizz lidini-llah, you'll reach **Madrassa** and the **Tomb of Al-Ghuri**. This splendid group of madrassa, mausoleum and wakalat was built by one of the last Mameluk sultans, Qansuh Al-Ghuri. The madrassa on the west has a covered cruciform plan and an unusual rectangular minaret topped with fine 'chimney pots'. Opposite, the mausoleum has lost its dome and is now used as a cultural centre. The Tomb of Al-Ghuri,

known as 'Al-Ghuri Palace', has been restored and is open to the public, complete with art exhibitions and a free folklore evening featuring a Whirling Dervish every Wednesday and Saturday.

From here, walk north a few steps and turn right to reach the **Wakalat Al-Ghuri**, a merchant's hostel built in the 16th century, which exhibits arts and crafts, many for sale.

A bit further on, turn left to reach **El-Azhar Mosque and University**, Islam's most prestigious place of learning. Its name means 'The Splendid', in Arabic, and there can be little doubt that its lofty gates and fairytale minarets capture the essence of Islamic architectural bravura. Begun in AD 970, the original Mosque of Fatima ez-Zahra (daughter of the Prophet Mohammed) was later expanded with minarets, gates, libraries, and hostels for pilgrims and students.

Wander through the sunny courtyard, fringed with hostel rooms, to the Great Chamber and there take a look at the two prayer niches. El-Azhar is still a university, attracting some 30,000 students from all over the Islamic world to study law, medicine and theology.

Negotiate tumultous traffic on El-Azhar Street to reach Cairo's renowned handicraft bazaar, **Khan El-Khalili**. A shopping trip here is a must for any visitor to Egypt, and yet this is more than a mere tourist bazaar. Cairenes are the main customers at tiny shops selling everything from priceless oriental jewellery to gimcracks and cheap household wares, genuine treasures to fake junk.

Many of the shops are themselves works of art, boasting ornate, wooden doorways and delicate traceries, floors of oriental carpets, and interiors redolent with the scent of cedar, sandalwood or incense.

Ask the shopkeeper for a tour of his workshops, and he may lead you on a labyrinthine chase to a crumbling room at rooftop level. There, watch the craftsmen hard at work on pounded copper, intricate inlay, or jewelled arabesques in silver and gold. Once you've observed the amount of

labour involved in creating any one of these handicraft items, you'll realize the prices are in fact quite moderate.

 Return to Muizz lidini-llah to get to the imposing **Kalawun Mosque** complex, which includes a hospital and madrassa (theological seminary), the mausoleum of Sultan Kalawun, and the mosque itself. The complex was finished in

1293, with its façade richly worked in the Islamic style, but reminiscent of the Crusader architecture brought from France. Be sure and visit the **Sultan's Mausoleum**, a discovery at the end of a dingy passageway, where a right turn leads through a soaring portal to the magnificent chamber. Note especially the fine carved and gilded ceiling, which is an outstanding incidence of the Moslem craftsman's art.

Rivalling Sultan Kalawun's pomp in the adjoining building is the 1836 **Madrassa of Sultan Berquq**. Passing the finely worked bronze doors, follow a hallway and turn right through more bronze doors, and you'll find yourself looking up at a canopy covered in gold arabesques on an azure background. A tip to the caretaker can open a door to the ornate tomb of Sultan Berquq's daughter.

Although it's only a short stroll from Berquq's Madrassa to the **Musafirkhana**, a guide is essential to lead you through the maze of narrow streets. Ask any neighbourhood child – he'll be only too pleased to

*S*tudents relax at El-Azhar University (left). Daughters of the rector used to watch them from this screened window (right).

help. Musafirkhana (from the Turkish for 'guest house') is a well-preserved mansion built in Mameluke style towards the end of the 8th century. Notice the intricately carved ceiling in the main salon.

Head back to Muizz lidinillah to see the restored **El-Aqmar Mosque**, dating from 1125, with its unusual façade. A few steps north and to the right stands **Bayt es-Suheimi**, home of the rector of El-Azhar two centuries ago. His house was divided into the two traditional sections of *salamlik* – where male guests were received – and *haramlik* – the private family quarters, where his wife and daughters lived. Off the main reception room is a chamber with huge chairs – symbols of the sheikh's great importance. Upstairs, stained glass, Turkish tiles and turned wooden screens (*mousharabiyeh*) transform the *haramlik* into a palace.

As you approach the northern wall of medieval Cairo, the great **Mosque of El-Hakim** stands out on the right. The mosque was finished in 1013 by the infamous mad caliph, El-Hakim. It has since been largely rebuilt and restored by the Bahara Moslem sect.

Nearby, the gates of Bab Al-Nasr and Bab Al-Futuh were part of the **city walls** erected at the end of the 11th century. These early walls have been much restored over the years, largely by Napoleon's troops less than two centuries ago. **27**

Names carved by soldiers in the stones of the towers and bastions can still be read. A guide will appear out of nowhere to sell you a ticket, lead you to the top of the wall, and show you where the town's defenders poured boiling oil on the heads of attackers.

THE CITADEL

From the centre of Cairo, the approach to the Citadel along El-Qalaa Street runs between two imposing mosques. The **Sultan Hassan Mosque**, finished in 1362, was a triumphal achievement for its builder and is considered by many to be the most beautiful mosque in the Middle East. The austere grandeur and extreme height of the main portal are matched by the four cavernous *iwans* (raised prayer areas) inside (all Persian-Turkish in style). Topping it off is the minaret, measuring 85m (267ft). Look behind the *mihrab* (prayer niche) for the **Tomb of Sultan Hassan**, with its pretty stained glass windows, an inscription band along its walls, and the striking squinches which support the dome. The tomb itself is constructed from Egyptian alabaster.

Across the road, the **Rifai Mosque**, finished in 1912, is the final resting place of scions of the house of Mohammed Ali. The Shah of Iran is also buried here – Egypt was the only country that would take the deposed leader.

Follow the road up to the **Citadel**, a massive Crusader-style fortress. Although dating in parts from Saladin's time (1207), its main building – the **Mosque of Mohammed Ali** (or 'Alabaster Mosque') – was only built in the early 19th century. The style is Ottoman baroque, with a few dashes of France's Louis Philippe, but the design is Turkish, with a colonnade surrounding a large, open forecourt. Even the pharaohs did not use alabaster as lavishly as Mohammed Ali: its

*T*he grand 14th-century Sultan Hassan Mosque is a masterpiece of Islamic architecture.

29

whole interior is covered in the creamy stone – although the pasha had his own tomb (to the right of the entrance) made from Carrara marble.

Behind the mosque there is a grand **panoramic view** of both Cairo and the Nile. Peer through the haze at the pyramids of Gîza looming in the distance on the edge of the desert. Then search the jumble of city blocks for the large, square court and ziggurat minaret of Ibn Tulun Mosque, a short distance west of the Citadel. It's your next stop.

Though a few Cairo mosques may be older, **Ahmed Ibn Tulun**'s is the best-preserved of the city's very early (AD 879) Islamic structures. Its

Ibn Tulun, builder of this well-preserved 9th-century mosque, died of an overdose of buffalo milk.

court, which is enclosed by a deep porch held up by five arcades, is the largest in Cairo (90m/300ft across); it is recognizable by the winding staircase outside its spiral minaret.

Next to the mosque, **Gayer-Anderson House** (Beit Al-Kreidleya), made up of two adjoining mansions, is one of Cairo's most fascinating museums, filled to the brim with oriental and western art. Major Gayer-Anderson was a British officer who bought the houses (built in 1540 and 1631), restored them, and then lived in them between the two World Wars. As well as being marvellous examples of traditional domestic architecture, they contain an excellent display of European, Arabic, Persian, Turkish and even Chinese decorative arts. They are open during normal museum hours (see p.131).

OLD CAIRO

Old Cairo, south of the modern city centre, can be reached by taxi; by metro from Tahrir Square to the Coptic Museum; or by crowded Nile River Bus from the jetty between Television Tower and the Ramses Hilton to the terminus at Masr El-Qadeema (Old Cairo).

Long before the founding of modern Cairo, it was here that the Romans had a fortress they called Babylon. The entrance to the old city is between two bulky Roman towers. Once inside the walls, you are surrounded by Coptic churches and monasteries from the early Christian era.

El Moallaqah, 'The Hanging Church', gets its unusual name from being built on top of two towers of a Roman city gate, with its mid-part 'hanging' between them. Although its foundations date from the 7th century, evidence seems to suggest that there was a church here even in the 4th century. Even so, its claim of being the oldest church in Egypt is contested by **Abu Serga Church** (St Sergius), where Mary, Joseph and Jesus are said to have taken shelter during their flight into Egypt. Abu Serga is deep in Old Cairo's back streets, lined with venerable doorways **31**

and paved with big, stone blocks rubbed smooth by the centuries. Glance up at the *mousharabiyeh* (screened windows), from where at least a dozen pairs of eyes watch your every movement.

Just a few steps from Abu Serga is the **Church of Saint Barbara**, decorated in typical Coptic style. Next door on the right is the small **Synagogue Ben-Ezra**, well restored due to overseas donations, but no longer used regularly for worship. The caretaker is proud of this historic synagogue and for a small contribution will show you the congregation's ancient holy books.

Before leaving Old Cairo, pay a visit also to the Coptic Museum (see p.35).

TWO ISLANDS

If you want to escape the bustle, spend some time on **Gezira Island**, with its sporting clubs, parks and the **Cairo Tower** (El-Borg), and cool off with a drink in the pleasant tea-garden at the tower's base. For a marvellous view, you can be whisked to the top of the 182m (600ft) tower.

*A*lthough prominent on the skyline, the Cairo Tower has not replaced the Pyramids as a symbol of Egypt.

Gezira is also home to Cairo's **opera house complex**, which houses the Modern Art Museum. At the southern tip of the island is the grand Gezira Sheraton Hotel (see p.67).

At the north end of **Roda Island** (slightly smaller than Gezira) is the **Manial Palace**, now a museum (see p.36). At the south end is Cairo's **Nilometre** (El-Miqyas), set up in the year AD 715 to indicate when the river would be at full flood. Now, the Aswân High Dam's careful control of the Nile's waters (see p.85) has made the Nilometre obsolete.

MUSEUMS

In the centre of Cairo, just north of Tahrir Square, is the **Egyptian Museum**, one of the most important museums in the world. It was built in the mid-19th century to house the wealth of artefacts discovered by successive waves of Egyptologists following the pioneers brought in by Napoleon Bonaparte. This immense collection contains treasures that reach back 5,000 years, and is most easily tackled by concentrating on just a few of the best items.

Beyond the lobby, once inside the museum proper, turn left and walk between the pairs of colossal statues to the **Old Kingdom Room**, with the collection's most ancient statues and sarcophagi. A small funerary chamber from Dahshur (6th Dynasty) has colourful walls engraved with the supplies provided for the dead man's celestial voyage, including a few jugs of beer.

Further on, notice the stylized but nonetheless intensely life-like statue (No. 141) of a scribe from Saqqara (5th Dynasty); its glass eyes catch the light with startling reality. In room 32, the realistic statues of **High Priest Ra-Hotep** and his wife **Nofret** (No. 223) suggest the considerable beauty of **33**

Tutankhamun's mask is the highlight amongst the treasures of the 19-year-old king.

which, in the exaggerated and naturalistic style of the period, reveal the king's fat thighs and distended belly.

Above the west stairs, visit the **War-and-Peace Exhibition**. Some of the most interesting artefacts come from the reign of Ramses II, including a huge, stone block representing the king's fist and symbolizing the weight of the pharaoh's authority. Also here are Ramses II's coffin, treasure cases, a number of beautiful exhibits from Amarna, and Tutankhamun's finely painted chest.

Illustrating the daily life of ancient Egyptians, in rooms 22, 27, 32 and 37 there are delightful wooden figures made as 'servants' for the dead, to provide for the honoured who departed this life in times past. Soldiers, craftsmen with toy tools, boatmen with a funeral ship, even ducks, fish, dogs

ancient Egyptian nobility, enhanced by clothing and cosmetics. The artist's magic also extended to animals – No. 446 (room 12) is a beautifully serene cow effigy, a symbol of the goddess Hathor. It was discovered in the shed on display behind it, which also has its own starry firmament.

In room 8, the gilded coffin lid with carnelians and blue glass, was created for Tutankhamun's brother. Room 3 is devoted to the reign of **Akhenaton**, with two giant statues,

and cattle – whole villages of figures found in single tombs.

One of the museum's most popular exhibits is **King Tutankhamun's treasure**. The king died mysteriously at the tender age of 19, and his half-finished tomb in the Valley of the Kings at Thebes (Luxor) (see p.81) was filled with an array of treasure unparalleled in its variety, exquisite beauty, and sheer weight of gold. Seeing this treasure of 1,700 items buried with a relatively minor king, it is incredible to imagine what the tombs of great pharaohs such as Ramses II must have contained. Sadly, only that of Tutankhamun escaped the ravages of centuries of grave-robbing, to be found intact by British archaeologist Howard Carter in 1922.

In room 4 are the best of the 'smaller' pieces, including a solid gold coffin, jewellery, and Tutankhamun's fabulous mask. The treasures are so numerous that they fill the nearby corridors and galleries: the bejewelled golden throne, bearing the sun-symbol of Aton; gold-plated cases, and a large, gold box surmounted by rows of sacred cobras and guarded by four gilded maidens. If you visit Tutankhamun's tomb, you will marvel that all this fitted into such a small space.

Also upstairs is the Mummy Room, diplaying a couple of dozen royal mummies in climatically controlled cases.

Next to the Egyptian Library, just off Ahmed Maher Square, is the **Museum of Islamic Art.** Despite the taboo on depicting human or animal figures – though you may spot a few exceptions – Moslem craftsmen showed remarkable versatility and finesse in their fashioning of prayer mats, illuminated manuscripts, stained glass, faience, and inlaid stone work. Also worth visiting is the arms collection, which includes daggers and swords set with precious stones, rifles and siege guns worked in silver, and deadly-looking poignards and scimitars.

The **Coptic Museum** is the centrepiece of Old Cairo (see p.31). Assembled here are fine examples of Coptic craftsmanship found in old churches and **35**

Stone carving from an old mansion in the Coptic Museum.

houses, notably wood, stained glass, *mousharabiyeh* screens and sculpted works. Similar to Islamic work, the delicate tracery used in illuminating Moslem holy books is also found in Coptic Bibles. Although Christianity permitted its artists to portray men and beasts, the main difference between Coptic and Islamic art seems to be in the former's sobriety, rather than freedom, of style.

The palace of Prince Mohammed Ali on Roda Island was converted into the **Manial Palace Museum** after the fall of the monarchy. Inside, pavilions and salons are filled with the luxuries and curiosities of royal daily life, from sparkling jewels and chandeliers to lustrous Turkish tiles and carpets. With its beautiful gardens, the complex is a pleasant refuge from the noise and dust of the city. The Club Méditerranée Hotel is also here (see p.67).

In the newly-renovated **Mohammed Mahmoud Khalil Museum**, close to the Cairo Sheraton Hotel, some fine examples of Impressionists such as Van Gogh and Gauguin are on display. Nearby at the **Papyrus Institute**, set up by Professor Hassan Ragab on a houseboat on the Nile, you can see papyrus being made, and buy the finished product. Further south (1km) is **Dr Ragab Pharaonic Village**, on Jacob Island. A barge-like 'amphitheatre' is towed along a papyrus-fringed canal, giving an insight into the industrial and agricultural work of ancient Egypt.

The Pyramids

GÎZA

The first surprise of Gîza's pyramids is to discover them, not isolated in the desert as you may imagine, but next to Cairo's southern suburbs, at the end of the Avenue of the Pyramids. It is somewhat incongruous to see these architectural marvels as they come into view beyond a mundane series of hotels and offices.

Abruptly, the desert begins, with the geometrical shapes, so perfect from afar, yielding their secrets of construction as you approach. Each pyramid is made from millions of massive, stone blocks, and their faces are in reality like giant staircases, not smooth, as they might appear at first. Without doors or windows to give them scale, their monolithic forms seem deceptively small until you arrive at the bases, from where these man-made mountains assert an overwhelming

Pyramids

The ideas that first-prompted the ancient Egyptians to start burying their dead under mounds are shrouded in the mysteries of time. Whatever the original motives, some of the most astounding structures ever constructed by man came to be developed from these first early piles of earth covered in bricks. It is said that 100,000 men laboured for 20 years to build the Great Pyramid of Cheops (see p.38).

The earliest tombs (*mastabas*) were rectangular and flat-topped. When Imhotep put several *mastabas* on top of one another for King Djoser's tomb, the idea caught on and the era of pyramid construction began. Many of the mammoth monuments seem uncomplicated in their basic architecture, but in fact, their simplicity conceals a whole world of intricate design intimately related to the religious beliefs of the early Egyptians.

force with their formidable, precise majesty.

The Gîza pyramids were the work of the Old Kingdom's 4th Dynasty, around 2600 BC. The largest of the three, the **Great Pyramid of Cheops**, towers at 137m (450ft), has almost 2½ million gigantic stone blocks, and is the only survivor of the Seven Wonders of the Ancient World. Climbing the façade (though tempting for a better look at Cairo and the Nile) is wearing (as well as dangerous) for both climber and pyramid, and is forbidden in any case. If visiting the interior of the Great Pyramid, you need to be non-claustrophobic to follow the guide into the eery depths of Cheops' funerary chamber, with its sarcophagus and ventilation shafts.

You can hire a camel between pyramids, or a horse-drawn carriage (*hantour*).

The **Pyramid of Chephren** is 0.6m (2ft) shorter than the Great Pyramid, but its position on higher ground makes it appear taller from a distance. The smooth-finished stones which were once a feature of almost all the pyramids can still be seen near the top. A tour of the interior here is slightly easier than at the Cheops pyramid, but still requires a guide.

The smallest of the three, the **Pyramid of Mykerinus**, (66m/216ft), was the last to be built at Gîza. Standing around them all are the immense *mastaba* tombs of the pharaohs' family, officials and nobles.

The **Sphinx** was sculpted in Pharaoh Chephren's image, to guard his tomb. In the ensuing 1,000 years it was buried by shifting sands. Thutmosis IV (1425–1408 BC) uncovered and restored the great beast, according to the inscription on a stele which stands between its paws. Some 3,000 years later, the Mamelukes aimed at the monument for artillery practice. In these more respectful times, the Sphinx is the subject of constant care and restoration, and is ever hopeful of reclaiming his nose from the British Museum in London.

Close by, the **Valley (Funerary) Temple of Chephren** is remarkable for its alabaster

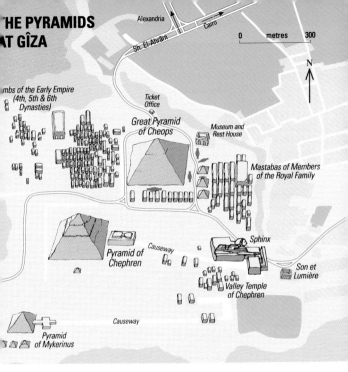

THE PYRAMIDS AT GÎZA

Alexandria

Cairo

Sh. El-Ahrâm

0 metres 300

N

Tombs of the Early Empire (4th, 5th & 6th Dynasties)

Ticket Office

Great Pyramid of Cheops

Museum and Rest House

Mastabas of Members of the Royal Family

Pyramid of Chephren

Causeway

Sphinx

Son et Lumière

Valley Temple of Chephren

Causeway

Pyramid of Mykerinus

floor and superb assembly of huge, smooth granite monoliths. Also of note is the **solar barque**, one of several Lebanese cedar longboats which were unearthed near the temple in 1954. The boat, made to bear Cheops' soul to the Other World, is in a small museum south of the Great Pyramid.

SAQQARA AND MEMPHIS

The road south from Gîza skirts fields watered by canals from the Nile and continues to **Saqqara**, the largest necropolis in Egypt, with hundreds of tombs and monuments erected in the course of ancient Egyptian history. Activity here was **39**

especially intense during the period of the Old Kingdom, when pharaohs had their capital at Memphis.

Look first at the **Step Pyramid of Djoser** (3rd Dynasty), the first of the great pyramids, built perhaps a century before those at Gîza. Imhotep, King Djoser's prime minister and a nobleman, is revered by architects as the first person to erect a monumental building made of stone. *Mastaba* tombs such as these were rectangles which were more or less modified to suit the tastes and budget of both builder and intended occupant.

To emphasize the power of his master, Imhotep stacked six large *mastabas* of diminishing size on top of one another and so created the Step Pyramid. A later king, Seneferou (4th Dynasty) produced a rhomboidal or bottom-heavy pyramid (which looks oddly bent when viewed from below) at Dahshur, which is visible from Saqqara to the south. It was Seneferou's son Cheops who perfected the design, and went on to construct the most impressive pyramid of all at Gîza (see p.38).

Several tombs surrounding the Step Pyramid boast exceptionally beautiful murals. The **mastaba of Princess Idut** (6th Dynasty) is at the end of the

The great Sphinx waits patiently for someone to reunite him with his nose and beard.

colonnade that you approach after buying your entry ticket. It is particularly rich in nautical scenes. Next to it is the small **Pyramid of Unas** (5th Dynasty), from where Dahshur can be seen. There are several names painted on the walls inside, including Ahmed the Carpenter, who recorded his break-in to the pyramid several centuries ago.

North east of the Step Pyramid, the **Tomb of Mereruka** (6th Dynasty) has 30 rooms decorated with scenes of hunting and fishing so precise in detail that zoologists were able to use them to study the wildlife of ancient Egypt. The murals in the **Tomb of Kagemni** (6th Dynasty) close by are equally fine, and have more colour preserved.

A short drive or walk north west of the Step Pyramid will bring you to the modest Rest-House named after Auguste Mariette, the French archaeologist who discovered many of the monuments in this area and founded Cairo's Egyptian Museum (see p.33). Take a camel ride or short walk across the

sands to the **Tomb of Ti** (5th Dynasty). This jewel among Old Kingdom tombs lay buried for 4,500 years until discovered by Mariette. Lord Ti served several pharaohs and, as a high court official, could call on the finest craftsmen and artists to embellish his tomb with animated friezes.

Just north of Ti's tomb is the **Serapeum** (also discovered by Mariette in 1850-51), in which sacred bulls were mummified and buried from the earliest times of Egyptian civilization right up to the Christian era.

On the way back to Cairo, stop off at the meagre but interesting ruins of **Memphis** on the Nile (16km/10 miles from Cairo), the great metropolis which remained the first city of Egypt until the end of the 6th Dynasty (around 2200 BC). The two principal relics are a colossal, recumbent limestone statue of Ramses II and a New Kingdom alabaster sphinx. A gigantic, red, granite statue of Ramses II has been removed from Memphis to stand adjacent to Ramses Square railway station in Cairo.

Alexandria and the Mediterranean

Alexandria (population 3 million), once a great capital, lies some 220km (137 miles) north of Cairo on the west of the Nile Delta. If the town, founded in 332 BC by Alexander the Great, has lost its monumental and cultural grandeur to war and careless modern construction, there is at least real pleasure in getting to know its independent-minded and spirited people – inhabitants of a place that is proudly separate from Cairo's bureaucracy.

The colourful members of this Levantine port's cosmopolitan community, celebrated in Lawrence Durrell's *Alexandria Quartet*, are only a distant memory since the 1952 revolution, and subsequent conflicts have driven the last of them away. Nostalgics might, however, return to their old haunts at the bar of the Cecil Hotel or the Pastroudis Café.

Alexandria's sights occupy only one full day, but it is worth an overnight stay just to enjoy a leisurely dinner at one of the many good fish restaurants on the seafront.

Start at the western end of the **Corniche**, which is officially known as 26 July Street and which hugs the sweeping curve of the eastern harbour. The coast road continues from the town centre right to Montazah Palace 8km (5 miles) to the east. On the peninsula, at a commanding position on the Corniche's western end, is the former royal palace of **Ras El-Tin**, which was built for Mohammed Ali in 1834-45.

Just east of the palace, part of the 15th-century **Fort of Qait Bey**, now a Naval Museum, stands on what was probably the site of Alexandria's Pharos lighthouse. One of the Seven Wonders of the Ancient

Alexandria's modern skyline would be a surprise to this lady at the Greco-Roman Museum. **43**

World, and the blueprint for all subsequent lighthouses around the world, it measured 180m (600ft) and was constructed of marble. After a look at naval battle relics of the Napoleonic Wars, stroll around the fort and enjoy the fine **view** of the city and harbour.

South of the Qait Bey Fort, just along from the Corniche, stands the impressive **Mosque of Abul Abbas** (1767). Continue to the centre of town to **Saad Zaghloul Square**, with its bustling bus-terminus. The square's café-terraces are good sport for people-watchers, as well as offering good views of the sea and bay.

Next, turn inland to visit the **Greco-Roman Museum**. Despite its name, it is also rich in pharaonic relics. Other fascinating reminders of the city's Greek and Roman past are the **Roman amphitheatre** at Kom Ed-Dikka, unearthed in 1963, and the nearby **Catacombs** of Kom Esh-Shugafa, which date from the early years of the Christian era (2nd century AD) and preserve an unusual mixture of both pharaonic and

Roman styles. Nearby, **Pompey's Pillar** actually has nothing to do with the redoubtable Roman invader, Pompey. The pillar – a 30m (95ft) monument shaped from rosy Aswân granite – was constructed long after Pompey's time, in honour of Emperor Diocletian in the 3rd century AD.

Continuing east, you reach Zizinia, with its popular **Jewellery Museum**. Housed in a Farouk family royal palace, its main attractions are an extravagant collection of jewels and equally grandiose bathrooms.

THE BEACHES

Although relatively undiscovered by tourists, the beach and nearby resorts along the coast here are where many Cairenes spend their summer holidays. Alexandria's beaches start in the centre of town, but many of the best are located to the east at **Maamoura**, **Montazah** and **Aboukir**. This last, which is at the site of Nelson's victory over Napoleon's fleet in 1798, is now more famous for its seafood than recreation.

West from Alexandria the Mediterranean coast stretches for some 500km (over 300 miles) to the Libyan frontier. There are several resorts along the way, all accessible by public transport. One particularly popular Egyptian resort, which is now practically an extension of Alexandria, is **Agami**.

A 90-minute drive (160km/ 100 miles) from Alexandria, is **El-Alamein**, which is now an attractive and peaceful beach resort, having earned its place in history as the theatre of the savage desert battles of 1942. **Cemeteries** of the war-dead from both sides and a **museum** commemorate the decisive victory of Montgomery's British Commonwealth forces over Rommel's German army. **Sidi Abdel Rahman**, 20km (12 miles) beyond the town, offers clear waters, and a fine beach and hotel.

A 2-hour drive (300km/185 miles) west from El-Alamein, close to the Libyan frontier, is

Enjoy a quiet moment on the beach at Montazah, a few minutes from downtown Alexandria.

Mersa Matruh, the area's administrative capital and main fishing port. In addition, it also offers a good selection of resort hotels and safe, sheltered beaches for both swimming and other watersports.

MONASTERIES OF WADI NATRUN

On the desert road returning from Alexandria to Cairo, take the chance to go to the **Coptic monasteries** at Wadi Natrun. (The region takes its name

from the natron mineral found here and used in mummification and making glass. Around 120km (75 miles) from Alexandria, turn right at the Rest-House to find the monasteries, which are a further 10km (6 miles) from the main road.

High walls, profound piety, and a simple ascetic life dominate the values of the monks at the monasteries of **Deir Anba Bishoi, Deir Anba Baramos, Deir Es-Suryani**, and **Deir Abu Makar**. This last was the most important of the ancient monasteries, and provided the Coptic church with most of its early leaders.

Monks have lived in seclusion here since the 4th century, and recent excavations led to the discovery of a headless skeleton, that some say could be that of St John the Baptist (his head is in the Omayyad Mosque in Damascus).

Fayyoum

Fayyoum is a large area (1,300 sq km/500 sq miles) of cultivation, which is irrigated by a canal from the Nile and surrounded by the Western Desert, under 2 hours' drive from Cairo. The land here is flat, with crops of almonds, apricots, oranges and lemons, and lush fields tilled by bullock-drawn plough or men wielding primitive mattocks.

Horse carts piled high with fodder, cane, or grass mats, or laden with passengers, rumble along the road, past women swathed in flowing black robes poised with heavily laden baskets balanced expertly on their heads. Here and there a palm grove offers welcome shade, or a picturesque water-wheel of time-darkened wood creaks slowly round.

Medinet El-Fayyoum, capital of the province, is a sizeable town of some 400,000 people. During Greek times it was known as *Crocodilopolis,* because it was sacred to the crocodile god, Sobek. Visitors crowd around the monumental water-wheels, which raise the waters of the Bahr Yusuf tributary of the Nile for the purposes of irrigation.

Lake Qaroun, about 16km (10 miles) north of Fayyoum, is well stocked with fish as well as being famous for hunting and duck shooting. On the southern shore, the old hunting lodge of the late King Farouk has now been converted into a hotel. Swimming in the lake is not recommended.

Amongst the pharaonic sites in Fayyoum, the ruined temple constructed by Amenemhat III at **Medinet Madi** is quite well preserved but difficult to get to, while the **Maidum**, **Lahun** and **Hawara** ruined pyramids are more accessible.

Most convenient of all – just off the Cairo desert road in a fascinating desert setting – are the remains of the Ptolemaic and Roman town of **Karanis**. These are located on an escarpment which overlooks the Fayyoum, and also incorporate an interesting museum, which houses Roman coins, jewellery, mummies, and the Fayyoum portraits.

47

Upper Egypt

South along the Nile's slender green valley, Egypt becomes increasingly more African and less Arabic. The rich sprawl of the delta gives way to an ever-narrowing fertile strip along each bank of the mighty river. The *fellahin* (peasants) compensate for the lack of land by intensive cultivation of what little they have. Crops of sugar cane and cotton overhang the riverbank, and oxen pull primitive ploughs, tow carts and turn water-wheels. Every conceivable type of pumping system devised by man since the dawn of time is pressed into service to irrigate the fields.

From dusty heaps of broken pottery to splendid temples, traces of pharaonic Egypt are to be found all along the journey. At **Abydos**, the votive **temple** to Osiris, which was built by Seti I (19th Dynasty),

The hypostyle hall leading to the inner sanctum of the Temple of Hathor at Denderah.

includes fine mural paintings – but tread carefully over the uneven floor of the shadowy rooms (a good pocket-torch is a must). Abydos was sacred to the memory of the beloved god Osiris who, after he was murdered and cut into pieces by his brother Seth, became king of the Nether World. Behind the great Seti temple is the **Osireion**, a cenotaph built by Seti I as a symbolic gesture to show his love for Osiris, although he arranged for his actual tomb to be in the Valley of the Kings at Thebes, where the pharaohs thought they would never be discovered (see p.82).

A 5-minute walk across the sand brings you to the ruined **Temple of Ramses II**, whose walls still bear traces of their once brightly blazing colours.

Further upriver is the temple complex at **Denderah**. Entering the main gate, on the right is the Roman birth-temple, or **Mammisi of Augustus**. The reliefs fail to match the artistry of Middle and New Kingdom monuments, but are interesting for their depiction of the birth and nourishment of an infant **49** god, symbolic of Egypt's ruler. The Mammisi of Nectanebo (30th Dynasty), another birth-temple, was built late in pharaonic times. Between the two Mammisi are the ruins of a Coptic church.

In the Denderah complex, the main temple is the **Temple of Hathor**, honouring Hathor, mother of the gods and wife of Horus. She is most often portrayed as a beautiful woman, crowned with graceful horns enclosing a solar disc, but she can also take the shape of a cow, symbol of fertility, and sometimes combines the attributes of both.

The columns in the hypostyle hall are topped by capitals bearing the face of Hathor. The offertory hall has similar columns and murals showing Hathor distributing her blessings. Further in, the sombre holy of holies is vaguely disquieting amid mystical bas-reliefs and the dust of ages. The more adventurous follow the caretaker down to narrow, low-ceilinged crypts to look at several other fine murals (and **50** a good collection of bats!).

The rooms above the holy of holies have murals showing the Egyptian process of embalming. Here the ceilings are framed by the sinuous body of the goddess Nut, who symbolized the sky. To escape the gloom of the inner sanctuaries, climb up to the temple roof, with its magnificent **view** of the surrounding hills.

The **Sacred Lake** is to the west, while behind stands the smaller **Temple of Isis**, who was sister and wife of Osiris, and mother of Horus.

LUXOR

From 2100-750 BC (10th-25th Dynasties), Egypt's power and glory were epitomized by the great temples of Luxor and Karnak (in what was then the city of Thebes). It was here that the New Kingdom (1570-1100 BC) revelled in its finest hour, with the city of the living thriving between the two temples, while the city of the dead, the Theban Necropolis, lay opposite on the Nile's west bank. With the Assyrian invasion in the 7th century BC, however,

14 centuries of grandeur ended abruptly, and for the Romans and Greeks, Thebes became simply a crumbling, but magnificent tourist attraction.

Later, even that went, when first the French and then a host of other European and American Egyptologists swept away centuries of dust from temples and tombs. With the opening of the Suez Canal (see p.94) in 1869, European interest in Egypt increased, and visitors quickly discovered the country's delightful winter climate. The monuments and temperatures of Luxor (current population 60,000) have been enjoyed ever since.

Divine Co-existence

Ancient Egypt's religion was a matter of divine profusion and confusion. Local gods merged attributes with one another and with gods from other areas, and no one was ever quite sure which was which. All appear to have been happy and benevolent, and no pressing need seems to have been felt to tidy up the pantheon. Some of the most popular gods are listed below.

Deity	Forms	Function
Amon-Ra	Sun, ram, hawk	Chief god, patron of Thebes
Osiris	Pharaoh	Underworld god
Isis	Beautiful woman	Sister-wife of Osiris; mother of Horus
Hathor	Cow, goddess with horns	Fertility, love, joy
Horus	Falcon, winged solar disc, infant	Sun god, protector of the king; plus many other functions
Anubis	Jackal	Funeral ceremonies god
Thoth	Ibis	Wisdom and learning
Ptah	Man	Creator, and teacher of skills and crafts
Maat	Ostrich plume	Justice

VALLEY OF THE KINGS

Tomb of Amenophis III

Tomb of Tutankhamun

Tombs of the Kings

Deir el-Bahari Temple of Hatshepsut

Pyramid Temple of Mentuhotep II

'Ilwet el-Sheikh 'Abd el-Gurnah

Site of Ramesside Temple

Temple of Thutmosis II

VALLEY OF THE QUEENS

Ptolemaic Temple

Temple of Thutmosis IV

Temple of Amenophis II

Ramesseum

NECROPOLIS OF THEBES

Tombs of the Queens

Deir el-Medineh

Medinet Habu (Ancient Town of Jeme)

Temple of Ramses III

Temple of Ramses

Temple of Thutmosis III

Pavilion of Ramses III

Colossi of Memnon (Amenophis III)

Site of Palace of Amenophis III

BIRKET HABU

(Site of Lake of Amenophis III)

N

0   0.5   1 km

0   0.25   0.5 miles

LUXOR / THEBAN NECROPOLIS / VALLEY OF THE KINGS

Esna

The town's long **Corniche** is bordered by trees, with Nile cruise boats moored alongside. Graceful *feluccas* offer a waterborne view of the town or a trip across river to the Valley of the Kings (see p.64). The great pillars of Luxor Temple, illuminated at night, dominate the eastern bank, an irresistible focus for an evening promenade. A week in this delightful atmosphere passes swiftly – a few days is barely enough to see the essentials.

Begin sightseeing at **Luxor Temple**. Amenophis III (18th Dynasty) and Ramses II (19th Dynasty) were the main builders of this building (1400 to 1250 BC), which, impressive as it may be, served only as the setting for the solemn New Year's pageant honouring the

chief god, Amon. During the ceremonies, Amon was represented variously as either the Sun God, Amon-Ra, or as the lascivious, outrageously demonstrative Amon-Min, a deity depicted with an impressive phallic image in several of the temple's murals.

In front of the great pylon (gateway) is a finely wrought **obelisk**. Originally there were two, but Mohammed Ali presented the other to France in 1831 and today it stands on the Place de la Concorde in Paris. Inside the great pylon, up to the left, the little Mosque of Abu'l Haggag is perched on pillars in Ramses II's court. A number of Coptic churches also once shared the temple grounds. Past the court, a monumental colonnaded way leads

*T*he processional avenue of sphinxes links Karnak to Luxor's Great Temple of Amon (above). **55**

to the older, inner court of Amenophis III.

Great though it is, Luxor Temple appears only 'minor' when compared to the awesome **Karnak Temple**, which for many is pharaonic Egypt's grandest monument of all. The **Great Temple of Amon** is in fact the largest of a vast complex of temples, sacred lakes, chapels and sphinx-lined triumphal ways stretching 3km (1.8 miles) along the Nile, and linking the Karnak and Luxor sanctuaries. A century of archaeological work has uncovered and reconstructed a vast proportion, but this is nonetheless only a fraction of all that was built during 1,400 years of Theban greatness.

The Great Temple was built, modified and then expanded according to pharaonic whim over a period of 2,000 years, from the Middle Kingdom to Roman times. The **first pylon** (which is what you see first), was in fact the last part built. As Egypt's biggest pylon, it was intended to be the Ptolemies principal contribution. It **56** was never finished, however,

and consequently lacks the traditional friezes recording the glories of the Ptolemy dynasty.

Behind the tremendous bulk of the 12m (40ft) thick pylon, there is an open space of about 8,000sq m (86,000sq ft) which constitutes the largest **court** of any Egyptian temple. Left of the entrance is the small Temple of Seti II (19th Dynasty); the one further along on the right is the work of Ramses III (20th Dynasty). Symbolizing the sun's journey through the celestial 'sea' was the sacred barque, which was mounted on the structure in the centre of the court.

The second pylon, which is guarded by two colossal statues of Ramses II, conceals one of the most formidable structures in the ancient world: the **great hypostyle hall**, where the tallest of 134 overpowering columns flank the centre aisle. Pause a while to take in the full effect and be amazed at how much of the original paint and decoration is still visible high up on the columns.

The third pylon, directly behind the great hypostyle hall,

dates from the time of Amenophis III (18th Dynasty, about 1400 BC). The narrow court in between the third and fourth pylons held four fine, granite obelisks, of which only one remains, although an even bigger obelisk – one of a pair erected past the fourth pylon

by Queen Hatshepsut – is the grandest of all. The fourth and fifth pylons, erected by Thutmosis I (18th Dynasty, about 1525 BC) are among the oldest parts of the temple.

Beyond the sixth pylon, the granite sanctuary is where the sacred barques were housed.

Egyptian Temples

Though each great temple is slightly different, all have a similar master plan. A mammoth gateway, or pylon, came first, and behind it was an open courtyard. A second pylon and courtyard followed. Next came a room called a 'hypostyle', filled with columns to support a roof. Another such room might follow, sometimes called the 'hall of offerings'. Finally, the inner sanctum, or 'holy of holies', was where the god 'lived' and where priests performed arcane ceremonies and sacred rites.

A typical temple plan might look like this:

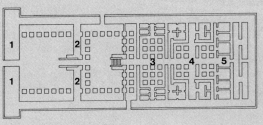

1. first pylon   3. hypostyle hall   5. holy of holies
2. second pylon   4. hall of offerings

Behind this is the oldest section of the great temple, part of a modest shrine erected in Middle Kingdom times.

Many parts of the immense, ruined temple area, with their piles of stones often hidden by high grasses, are difficult to identify without an elaborate archaeological plan. There is no missing the **Sacred Lake**, however, which is just south of the Great Temple of Amon. As part of the temple's ceremonial, sacred barques were set afloat on the lake to symbolize the daily celestial journey of Amon-Ra, the Sun God. Behind the lake to the east are the seats for the evening sound-and-light show. At the northern corner of the Sacred Lake is a very un-pharaonic (but vital) refreshment stand.

In late afternoon, visit the superb little **Luxor Museum** north of the Etap Hotel, which is air-conditioned and, compared to the jumbled Egyptian Museum in Cairo (see p.33), incredibly easy to get around. Two highlights of this compact collection are a striding basalt statue of Thutmosis III (No. 2)

and an unusual sandstone bust of Amenophis IV (Akhenaton, No. 53). In the new Cachette Hall, an alabaster Sphinx and the enthroned gods of Amon and Mut are amongst spectacular recent finds.

At the end of the afternoon, take a stroll through the town of Luxor, when the bazaars are still filled with life but not too crowded. At sunset, head for a Nile-side café, notably the terrace at the Winter Palace Hotel or others further along towards Luxor Temple.

THEBAN NECROPOLIS

The Valley of the Kings (see p.64) shelters the fabled tombs of the pharaohs, including the comparatively modest but best known one which belonged to Tutankhamun. It is only, however, one of a number of valleys which make up Thebes' vast 'city of the dead' on the west bank of the Nile. Tombs of royalty, nobles, court officers and the artisans who created the capital's monuments number in the hundreds, and there are also a dozen temples scattered throughout the necropolis. You could not possibly do justice to these marvels in a single day, so plan at least two days for touring the major sights on the west bank.

From dawn to late afternoon motorized ferryboats ply the Nile between the Savoy Hotel dock, the Winter Palace dock, and the west bank. Buy your return ferry ticket on the east bank, and your tickets to one or more of the temples and tombs from the booth at the west bank dock. Don't set off without them. Taxis and donkeys are always available for hire near the ticket-booth.

When you get to the tombs, be prepared for an occasional delay – the tombs tend to be small, but the crowds are not. Some tombs are lit, but in others caretakers illuminate the interiors by using an arrangement of mirrors, which quite literally throw light on darkness thanks to a reflected beam of sunlight. In several smaller tombs, numbers are restricted to protect the murals. Sometimes tombs are occasionally closed for restoration work.

From the dock, a road heads inland through lush irrigated farmland. Around 2.5km (1.5 miles) along, towards the ragged mountains, a pair of mammoth, seated figures rise from the midst of a field: the celebrated **Colossi of Memnon**. Their temple was ruined long ago by earthquakes, but 3,000 years later, these two gargantuan figures of Pharaoh Amenophis III sit, hands on knees, now serving as guardians of precious farmland just a few hundred yards from the desert. Towering 18m (60ft) above the ground, their fingers alone are over 1m (3ft) long.

West of the Colossi, a complex of temples is named after the modern Arabic village of **Medinet Habu** nearby, while beyond a mudbrick wall are the pylons of two temples. The first, begun in the 18th Dynasty under Amenophis I, is small but more harmonious in style than the one behind it, which is impressive in size but somewhat ponderous, and was built by Ramses III (20th Dynasty) some 350 years later. The relief decoration on the **59** latter is deeply carved for dramatic effect, but to some the result is rather coarse. Cleaning has revealed a surprising amount of surviving colour.

From Medinet Habu, a road runs directly to the **Valley of the Queens**. There are close to 80 tombs here which sheltered the remains of both queens and royal children. The **tomb of Prince Amon-her-Khopeshef** (20th Dynasty) (No. 55) preserves fine paintings with astonishingly bright colours, in particular the blues and yellows. After extensive restoration, precious tombs such as that of **Queen Nefertari** (wife of Ramses II – the finest of the tombs here) (No. 66), have recently been reopened to the public. You should also be able to see the **tomb of Prince Kha'emwaset** (No. 44) and that of **Queen Tyti** (No. 52).

Turn left on returning from the Valley of the Queens to reach the necropolis of **Deir el-Medineh**. Of the hundreds of tombs found both in and around this modern village, No. 1 is of particular interest. It belonged to Sennejem, a

This giant head of Ramses II has lain here since an earthquake toppled his Ramesseum temple.

high official of the 19th Dynasty, and its paintings have retained an amazing freshness of colour. As you descend, beware of the broken stairway and the small rock-hewn entrance. Nearby, tomb No. 359, of Inherka (20th Dynasty) is filled with paintings of gorgeous, sloe-eyed goddesses.

Although Ramses II (1304–1237 BC) achieved renown for erecting awesome monuments, his tomb in the Valley of the Kings is a little disappointing. Nonetheless, the funerary temple which he built to his own memory by the cultivated land remains a stupendous architectural achievement.

Called the **Ramesseum**, it was in fact a sprawling collection of palaces, temples and storerooms. Although ruined now, the scale of the temple and the score of huge statues of Ramses still make a great

impression. The present entrance to the ruins leads to the second court past four pillars (to your left), each with fine Osiride statues of the pharaoh. Beyond lies a great bulk of ruined stone which formed a colossal seated figure reaching 17m (55ft) high and weighing over 1,000 tons.

On the hillside behind the Ramesseum is the **Sheik Abd el-Gurnah** necropolis, named after the neighbouring village. The best of these tombs date right back to the 18th Dynasty – a heyday of ancient Egyptian creativity. The small **tomb of Nakht** (No. 52), who was a temple astronomer, depicts all the Nile's abundance in beautiful scenes of fruit gathering, reaping and wine-making. In the nearby **tomb of Mena** (No. 69), the colours are just as beautiful, although somewhat weakened in impact due to the protective glass plates.

Up the hillside, the **tomb of Sennefer** (No. 96) is worth the climb – the colours are amazingly well preserved and the uneven ceiling is charmingly decorated with grapevines. **61**

In the revealing **tomb of Rekhmire** (No.100) – which stands as a magnificent monument to the power wielded by this early Mayor of Thebes – murals show foreign ambassadors bringing offerings of baboons and monkeys, leopards, giraffes, ivory tusks and produce. Vignettes of Theban life also illustrate farmers and craftsmen producing goods to offer to the great Amon.

Ramose's Tomb (No. 55), is equally imposing, but was never finished. This high official's pharaoh, Amenophis IV (Akhenaton), carried out a religious revolution while work was in progress, and the tomb was abandoned when pharaoh and court both transferred operations down the Nile to Tell el-Amarna. The bas-reliefs are exceptionally fine. Girls with plaited hair and delicate features were carved with considerable skill, but were then left unpainted, giving the exquisite effect of engraving rather than bas-relief. A few figures strikingly outlined in black help to reveal the first stages in the painting process.

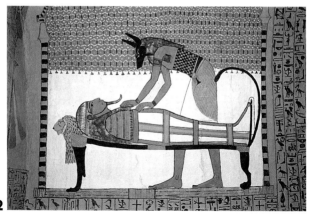

For yet another aspect of Theban artistry, visit the **tomb of Khaemhat** (No. 57), for its rare collection of several statues of its owner and his family. The nearby tomb of Userhet (No. 56) is also worth a visit.

The artistic brilliance of the 18th Dynasty reaches a high point in the temples of **Deir el-Bahari** (west of the main road), the greatest being that belonging to Queen Hatshepsut. When Thutmosis II died in 1505 BC, Thutmosis III, the new pharaoh, and the illegitimate son of Thutmosis II, was a mere boy. Queen Hatshepsut, his stepmother, consequently acted as regent, consolidating all power in her own hands. She became used to wielding the royal crook and scourge, symbols of the pharaoh's authority, and took to wearing the male ruler's costume and even the traditional stylized beard. She ruled for 22 years until her death, at which time Thutmosis III took his rightful place, reigning until 1450 BC.

Influenced by the tiered design of the nearby older temple of Mentuhotep II, the great **Temple of Hatshepsut** is an astounding monument. Constructed as a series of terraces on a grand scale, with stark colonnades blending in with the grooved mountainside rising behind, it is dedicated to the goddess Hathor, as can be seen in the murals' ubiquitous image of her sacred cow. Notice the particularly well-preserved paintings in the rooms behind the colonnade on the second terrace. At the southwest (left) end, the ceiling in the Chapel of Hathor is both as starry and blue as any nighttime Egyptian sky, while the yellow hues are as bright as reflected sunlight.

On the way to the Valley of the Kings, stop at Gurnah for a look at the funerary **Temple of Seti I** (19th Dynasty), father of Ramses II. Little remains of the temple's first two pylons and courts, but the hypostyle hall has many scenes showing **63**

Jackal-headed Anubis, god of the dead, mummifying a pharaoh in the Valley of the Kings.

Seti I and his son Ramses II making offerings to Thebes' great god, Amon.

 VALLEY OF THE KINGS

The timeless and craggy landscape of the Nile's west bank, where the sun descends nightly through the Nether World, seems the natural site for the pharaohs to pick as their eternal resting place. Undisturbed by the annual rising of the Nile waters, and hidden away in rock-hewn sepulchres behind secret, sealed entrances, they were well fitted out for their underworld journey. The provisions supplied in each tomb included furnishings and costumes, mummiform statues or small carved figures to act as servants and concubines, and food and drink. In addition the royal voyagers were given a detailed guidebook to the dangers of the celestial journey – a copy of the Book of the Dead was a standard accessory.

At the end of the trip, they submitted to the judgement of the divine Osiris, who would enlist the aid of Anubis and Thoth, gods of funeral rights and wisdom. Each pharaoh's heart was weighed in a balance against a feather, and if it was not heavy with sin, the pharaoh could enjoy a pleasant life in the land of Osiris. Back in Egypt, he would assume the aura of a deity, like a lesser Osiris, and family and subjects would worship him in his funerary temple.

A pharaoh began work on his elaborate tomb and funeral equipment as soon as he came to power. In spite of this foresight, many monarchs had the misfortune to die before preparations were completed. They were immediately sealed up in their imperfect tombs and the country's best artisans and craftsmen then marched off to begin work on the new king's tomb. Though tombs might be guarded for centuries, and the entrances lost to living memory, the grave-robbers' ingenuity increased according to the richness of the spoils. Since the time of the New Kingdom, thieves have been successful in breaking into every known tomb – with one exception.

A Selection of Egyptian Hotels and Restaurants

Recommended Hotels

The hotels below cover all major Egyptian destinations. Prices will vary according to season, travel agent's package and inflation. For booking directly, we include telephone and, where possible, fax numbers. (See p.138 for international telephone/fax codes.) Egyptian addresses are often inconsistent, with one hotel listed at apparently different locations. For consistency, we standardize addresses throughout.

At last inspection, the following hotels met reasonable standards of cleanliness and comfort, with air-conditioning usually available in all but the cheapest rooms. Following local practice, we quote prices in US dollars. (See p.130 for Nile cruises on floating hotels.) We have used the following symbols for a double room with bath per night:

▌	below $40
▌▌	$40–$80
▌▌▌	above $80

CAIRO

Atlas Zamalek ▌▌▌
20 Gamaet El Dowal Al Arabia Street, Mohandessin
Tel. 346 4175, fax 347 6938
Good, small hotel in chic neighbourhood, popular with the Middle Eastern bourgeoisie; renowned Tamango nightclub. 74 rooms.

Cairo Marriott Hotel ▌▌▌
Saraya El-Gezira Street, Zamalek
Tel. 340 8888, fax 340 6667
Khedive Ismail's palace, built for the opening of the Suez Canal; renovated with Oriental carpets, grand artwork. 1,147 rooms and bungalows, swimming pool, tennis courts, gardens, shops, casino, terrace restaurant, business centre.

Cairo Sheraton ▌▌▌
Galaa Square, Dokki
Tel. 348 8600, fax 348 9051
Twin towers on the west bank of the Nile with 660 rooms, circular swimming pool, casino, Oriental nightclub, restaurant with views of the pyramids, and business centre.

Carlton Hotel ▌
21 July 26th Street, Ezbekiya
Tel. 575 5181
Modest, old-fashioned charm in bustling city-centre. 60 rooms.

Gezira Sheraton ▯▯▯

Gezira Island
Tel. 341 1333, fax 341 3640
Round tower dominating the south end of Gezira Island with its 27 floors, offering superb views of both river and city, as well as 520 rooms, swimming pool, riverfront restaurants, casino, and a first-class business centre.

Grand Hotel ▯

17 July 26th Street, Ezbekiya
Tel. 575 7700, fax 575 7593
Amid the downtown bustle, this is an amiable hotel with 97 rooms, most of them large with balcony and old-fashioned furnishings.

Heliopolis Mövenpick ▯▯▯

Airport Road, Heliopolis
Tel. 291 9400, fax 667 374
Close to airport, but the 412 rooms are well soundproofed. European and Egyptian cuisine, swimming pool, shops, disco, and efficient business centre.

Manial Palace (Club ▯▯ Méditerranée) Hotel

Kasr Mohammed Ali, El-Manial
Tel. 844 524, fax 363 1737
On Roda Island in Manial Palace gardens, offering Club Méditerranée's 190 rooms and bungalows, with giant swimming pool and an equally mammoth buffet.

Mena House Oberoi ▯▯▯

Pyramids Road, Gîza
Tel. 383 3222, fax 383 7777
Situated in 16ha (40 acres) of gardens beside the pyramids, this hotel was built in 1869, but has since been renovated and expanded, with the result that the older part is more charming than the new. With 520 rooms, casino, Indian restaurant, swimming pool, horse riding, tennis, golf, good business centre. 20 minutes from downtown Cairo.

Le Méridien ▯▯▯

Corniche El-Nil, Garden City
Tel. 362 1717, fax 362 1927
Affording superb Nile views from the northern end of Roda Island, Le Méridien offers 275 comfortable rooms, a good (and popular) French restaurant, well-equipped health club, swimming pool, and a fine business centre.

Nile Hilton ▯▯▯

Tahrir Square
Tel. 765 666, fax 760 874
A Cairo institution, which is convenient for the Egyptian Museum just next door, and which boasts a good view of the pyramids from its restaurant. Offering 434 rooms (many of them riverside), swimming pool, casino, and good business centre.

67

Ramses Hilton

1115 Corniche El-Nil, Maspero
Tel. 777 444, fax 757 152
This 36-storey tower with grand riverside views occupies a central location, and is separated by a highway from the downtown area. The Ramses offers 849 rooms, casino, swimming pool, and first-class business centre.

Semiramis Intercontinental

Corniche El-Nil, Garden City
Tel. 355 7171, fax 356 3020
Great riverside views from this centrally located tower, which is built on the site used by the British as their headquarters during World War II. The Semiramis is an efficient complex consisting of 840 rooms, outdoor swimming pool, French cuisine, disco, good business centre and shops.

Shepheard's Hotel

Corniche El-Nil, Garden City
Tel. 355 3900, fax 355 7284
This is a modern riverside construction named after the original Shepheard's Hotel in Cairo which burnt down in 1952. Today's Shepheard's comes complete with 281 rooms with good views of Gezira Island, European and Middle Eastern cuisine, swimming pool, and business-centre.

Les Trois Pyramides

229 Pyramids Road, Gîza
Tel. 582 2233, fax 582 3700
A modern hotel, convenient for the pyramids, with 230 rooms in a 12-storey building, as well as a swimming pool and health club.

ALEXANDRIA AND THE MEDITERRANEAN

Beau Site

El Shatee Street, Marsa Matruh
Tel. 934 012, fax 933 319
Seafront family resort hotel. 103 rooms, good restaurant.

Hotel El-Alamein

Sidi Abdel Rahman, El-Dabaa Centre, El-Alamein
Tel. 492 1228, fax 492 1232
This handsome beach resort hotel is situated near the historic battlefield of the same name. Offering 209 rooms/chalets, beachfront gardens, tennis, swimming pool, and a variety of watersports.

Montazah Sheraton

Corniche Road, Montazah, Alexandria
Tel. 548 0550, fax 540 1331
A giant hotel situated opposite King Farouk's old palace; offering 305 rooms, a good seafood restaurant, swimming pool, efficient business centre.

Palestine Hotel   ❏❏❏
Montazah, Alexandria
Tel. 547 4033, fax 547 3378
In beautiful royal gardens beside the harbour, offering 208 rooms, swimming pools, business centre.

Pullman Cecil Hotel   ❏❏
16 Saad Zaghloul Square,
El-Ramleh, Alexandria
Tel. 807 055, fax 483 6401
Friendly, old-fashioned downtown landmark. 86 rooms, nightclub, casino, health club, good people-watching café, business centre.

San Giovanni Hotel   ❏
205 El-Gueish Street, Stanley
Tel. 546 7774, fax 546 4408
Cosy seafront hotel with 30 rooms and a good seafood restaurant.

LUXOR

Akhetaton Village   ❏❏
Khaled Ibn El-Walid Street
Tel. 580 850, fax 580 879
Club Méditerranée's 144-room resort hotel, superb swimming pool, disco and good shopping facilities.

Etap Luxor   ❏❏
Corniche El-Nil
Tel. 580 944, fax 383 316
Riverside hotel near Luxor Temple, museum and market, with 306 rooms, swimming pool, and disco.

Horus Hotel   ❏
Karnak Temple Street
Tel. 372 165
Small hotel near Karnak Temple at north end of town. 25 rooms.

Isis Hotel   ❏❏❏
Khaled Ibn El-Walid Street
Tel. 372 750, fax 382 923
Giant riverfront hotel at south end of town. 500 rooms, swimming pool, efficient business centre.

Luxor Hilton   ❏❏❏
New Karnak
Tel. 374 945, fax 374 946
Near Karnak Temple, with pretty gardens beside the river promenade. 261 rooms, swimming pool, casino and disco.

Luxor Sheraton   ❏❏❏
El-Awameya Road
Tel. 374 544, fax 374 941
Located in landscaped riverfront gardens at the south end of town. 298 rooms and bungalows, poolside grill restaurant, good business centre and shopping mall.

Mövenpick Jolie Ville   ❏❏❏
Crocodile Island
Tel. 384 855, fax 384 936
In a quiet garden location 7 km (4 miles) from the town centre. 320 rooms, tennis, sailing, swimming pool, and esteemed restaurant.

69

Savoy Hotel

El-Nil Street
Tel. 580 522, fax 581 727
Modest but clean riverfront hotel offering 108 rooms and air-conditioned bungalows.

Sophitel Winter Palace

Corniche El-Nil
Tel. 580 422, fax 374 087
Grand, old-fashioned hotel next to Luxor Temple, with Edwardian atmosphere bar, terrace overlooking exotic gardens, and a swimming pool. 370 rooms supplemented by the modern and less charming annex, the New Winter Palace.

ASWÂN

Amoun Hotel

Amoun Island
Tel. 480 444, fax 322 555
Club Méditerranée island-hotel in pleasant gardens facing Cataract. Felucca-ferry to town. 56 rooms, swimming pool.

Aswân Oberoi

Elephantine Island
Tel. 323 455, fax 323 485
Giant tower at the north end of Elephantine Island, with fine view of other islands and Cataract, and own excursion boats. 244 rooms, swimming pool.

Happi Hotel

Abtal El-Tahrir Street, Aswân
Tel. 322 028
Set back from Nile, the Happi is popular amongst backpackers, offering 60 rooms, some with a view of the river.

Isis Island Hotel

Isis Island
Tel. 315 100, fax 315 500
A sizeable, luxury bungalow resort on Isis Island, complete with 406 comfortable rooms, a swimming pool, health club, tennis and squash courts, and disco.

New Cataract Hotel

Abtal El-Tahrir Street, Aswân
Tel. 323 434, fax 323 510
Located next to the Pullman Cataract (see below), with 144 rooms in a comfortable block, and a good business centre.

Sofitel New Cataract Hotel

Abtal El-Tahrir Street, Aswân
Tel. 316 000, fax 323 222
A splendid British monument with impressive Moorish architecture; the 136 rooms at the Pullman Cataract have been renovated, but the hotel has nonetheless retained its colonial charm (enjoy a drink on the grand terrace looking over to Elephantine Island).

ABU SIMBEL

Nefertari Hotel

Abu Simbel
Tel. 316 403, fax 316 404
Near the temples, with air-conditoned rooms and swimming pool.

THE OASES

El-Khârga Oasis

El-Khârga, El-Wadi El-Guedid
Tel. 93766
Simple, modern establishment, 30 rooms, pleasant little garden.

Mebarez Tourist Hotel

2 El-Tharwa El-Khadraa Street,
El-Dakhla Oasis
Tel. 941 4524
Downtown and modern, with 27 rooms and restaurant, and convenient for bus to Farâfra.

RED SEA

Magawish Tourist Village

Magawish, Hurghada
Tel. 442 620, fax 440 255
Formerly a Club Méditerranée resort, and now government-run in the same style, with 314 bungalow-rooms, swimming pool, fishing, diving and other watersports facilities, a good seafood restaurant, and disco.

Menaville Hotel

Safâga
Tel. 451 761, fax 451 765
A sprawling resort complex with 152 rooms, shopping centre, European and Egyptian cuisine, swimming pool, tennis, watersports.

Sheraton Hurghada

Hurghada
Tel. 443 975, fax 442 831
125 luxury resort rooms, restaurants, swimming pool, watersports.

Sonesta Beach Resort

Hurghada
Tel. 443 661, fax 443 660
Cheerful village-like complex, offering 132 rooms, and good diving and fishing opportunities.

SUEZ CANAL

Etap Forsan Island

Ismailiya
Tel. 222 922, fax 222 220
On a Lake Timsah island, linked to the mainland by causeway. 152 rooms, sports facilities, swimming pool, and business centre.

Helnan Port Said

El Corniche Street, Port Said
Tel. 220 893, fax 223 762
A giant, modern waterfront hotel, offering 203 rooms and good business facilities.

Red Sea Hotel
13 Riad Street, Port Tawfik, Suez City
Tel. 223 334, fax 227 761
Quiet, port view. 81 rooms, seafood restaurant, business centre.

SINAI

Daniela Village
St Catherine
Tel. 749 772, fax Cairo 360 7750
Modest, clean, handy for St Catherine's Monastery and mountain. 42 rooms, restaurant.

Hilton Fairouz Village
Na'ama Bay, Sharm El-Sheikh
Tel. 760 575, fax 770 726
Resort complex: 150 rooms, good diving, fishing, tennis, squash, riding, fine seafood restaurant.

Mövenpick Sharm El-Sheikh
Na'ama Bay, Sharm El-Sheikh
Tel. 600 100, fax 600 111
Relaxed atmosphere, 210 rooms, good restaurants, swimming pool and all watersports.

Novotel Dahab Hotel
Dahab
Tel./fax 770 788
Between mountains and sea, 141 rooms, shopping mall, swimming pool, watersports, tennis, riding.

Novotel Sharm El-Sheikh Hotel
Sharm El-Sheikh
Tel. 600 179, fax 600 177
Family resort, 152 rooms, shopping, tennis, swimming pool, watersports, seafood restaurant.

Nuweiba Holiday Village
Nuweiba
Tel. 770 393, fax Cairo 762 701
Simple, friendly service, beachfront bar and restaurant.

St Catherine's Village
Wadi El-Raha, St Catherine
Tel. 770 456, fax 770 221
Superbly designed in local granite, with spectacular views of Mount Sinai, and close to St Catherine's Monastery. 100 chalets, gardens, tennis, panoramic restaurant.

Salah El-Deen Hotel
Taba
Tel. 771 345, fax Cairo 356 4005
Beside Pharaoh's Island, with 50 rooms, chalets, seafood restaurant.

Taba Hilton
Taba Beach, Taba
Tel. 763 544, fax 747 044
Mammoth resort hotel on Israeli border. 326 rooms, private beach, swimming pool, tennis, variety of restaurants, good business centre.

Recommended Restaurants

We appreciated the food and service in the restaurants listed below, but would welcome other recommendations. Pride of place goes to Middle Eastern cuisine, but for variety, we include Italian, French, Indian and other Oriental establishments.

Apart from some in Cairo and Alexandria, most restaurants are attached to major hotels which welcome non-residents. We note as 'formal' a few places which ask men to wear jackets, and we also note some which do not serve alcohol. The symbols below are intended as a guide to the price of a meal for one, excluding drinks:

	below $10.
	$10–$15
	above $15

CAIRO

Abou Shakra

69 Kasr El-Aini Street
Tel. 848 811, 848 602
Simple Egyptian fare, kebabs and kofta, friendly service, no alcohol.

Abu Aly's

Nile Hilton, Tahrir Square
Tel. 767 444
Café-terrace serving good, spicy Egyptian snacks and om ali dessert; good for people-watching.

Al Fanous

5 Wissa Wassef,
Riyadh Tower, Gîza
Tel. 737 592
Refined Moroccan cuisine served in an Oman restaurant complex. No alcohol.

Andrea

59 El-Maryoutia Canal Road,
Pyramids
Tel. 387 1133
Renowned for barbecued chicken on a spit, or grilled pigeon.

Arabesque

6 Kasr El-Nil Street
Tel. 759 896
First-class Egyptian cuisine – try molokhia soup and bamia lamb – and European dishes, in a pleasant art-gallery setting.

Asio House

Shepheard's Hotel,
Corniche El-Nil
Tel. 355 3800
Good Chinese and Indian cuisine, served with great courtesy in this charming hotel (see p.68).

73

Ba'albek 🔲🔲🔲
Sonesta Hotel, 4 El-Tayaran
Sreet, Heliopolis
Tel. 262 8111
Good Lebanese cuisine, mezzeh, and lively entertainment.

Bawadi 🔲🔲
10 Hussein Wassef Street, Dokki
Tel. 348 4878
Wide variety of first-rate Lebanese and Middle Eastern cooking.

Le Champollion 🔲🔲🔲
Le Méridien Hotel,
Corniche El-Nil, Garden City
Tel. 362 1717
This flagship hotel's French restaurant, named after Jean-François Champollion, the Frenchman who cracked the hieroglyphic code (see p.81), serves haute cuisine to classical music. Formal.

Chandani 🔲🔲
5 Wissa Wassef,
Riyadh Tower, Gîza
Tel. 737 592
Indian and Chinese cuisine in the Oman complex. No alcohol.

Christo 🔲🔲
10 Pyramid Street, Gîza
Tel. 383 3582
Near the pyramids, specializing in seafood – grilled or fancy Egyptian-style.

Ciao Italia 🔲🔲
Gezira Sheraton, Gezira Island
Tel. 341 1333
A romantic riverfront Italian restaurant in the celebrated hotel (see p.67), open for dinner only.

Citadel Grill 🔲🔲🔲
Ramses Hilton,
1115 Corniche El-Nil, Maspero
Tel. 744 400
Smart supper-club atmosphere for steaks and seafood. Formal.

Club Med Restaurant 🔲🔲
Manial Palace Hotel,
Kasr Mohammed Ali, El-Manial
Tel. 844 524
Club Med's classic gargantuan buffet offers Egyptian and French dishes in a charming garden.

Dahan 🔲🔲
Meshhet Al Hussein,
Khan El-Khalili
Celebrated Middle Eastern grill in the heart of market land. Popular with political and showbiz celebrities, many of whom come for the lamb kofta and kebabs.

Dragon 🔲🔲🔲
Gezira Sheraton, Gezira Island
Tel. 341 1333
Elegant riverfront restaurant, serving classical Chinese cuisine, open for dinner only.

El-Arze 🔘🔘🔘
Nile Hilton, Tahrir Square
Tel. 767 444
Garden service for Lebanese grill.

El-Nil Rôtisserie 🔘🔘🔘
Nile Hilton, Tahrir Square
Tel. 767 444
International cuisine and live classical music in elegant surroundings. Formal.

El-Omda 🔘
6 El-Gazzar Street, Mohandessin
Tel. 347 8652
Authentic Egyptian peasant fare. No alcohol.

Falafel 🔘🔘🔘
Ramses Hilton,
1115 Corniche El-Nil, Maspero
Tel. 744 400
Refined Middle Eastern cuisine along with a spectacular show. Dinner only.

Felfela Garden 🔘
15 Hoda Sharawi Street
Tel. 392 2833, 392 2751
Simple Egyptian cuisine in charming oasis-like décor.

Flying Fish 🔘🔘
166 El-Nil Street, Agouza
Tel. 349 3234
Egyptian-style seafood and traditional dishes.

The Grill 🔘🔘🔘
Semiramis Intercontinental,
Corniche El-Nil, Garden City
Tel. 355 717
Well-presented French cuisine – steaks, lamb, excellent seafood, with unobtrusive piano accompaniment. Dinner only.

Le Grill Gezira 🔘🔘🔘
Cairo Marriott Hotel, Saraya
El-Gezira Street, Zamalek
Tel. 340 8888
French cuisine in grand style. Live classical music.

Justine's 🔘🔘🔘
4 Hassan Sabry Street, Zamalek
Tel. 341 2961, 340 7510
French cuisine, popular with the Cairo élite. Formal.

Kandahar 🔘🔘
3 Gamaet El Dowal Al Arabia
Street, Mohandessin
Tel. 344 3773
A first-class Indian restaurant, sister establishment to the Oberoi's Moghul (see p.76).

Kebabgy 🔘🔘
Gezira Sheraton, Gezira Island
Tel. 341 1333
A popular hotel restaurant serving very good grilled Egyptian cuisine, accompanied by traditional Arab music in the evening.

75

Khan El-Khalili

5 El-Badistan Lane,
Khan El-Khalili
Tel. 903 788
Air-conditioned haven for foot-sore bazaar visitors. Put your feet up and enjoy the traditional Egyptian meals and snacks.

Kowloon

Cleopatra Hotel,
2 Abdel Salam Araf Street
Tel. 759 831
Wide variety of Chinese, Korean and Japanese dishes.

Madura

Cairo Sheraton,
Galaa Square, Dokki
Tel. 348 8700
Savoury Indonesian cuisine, nasi and bami goreng. Dinner only.

Mashrabia

4 Ahmed Nassim Street,
Orman Garden, Gîza
Tel. 348 2801, 348 3501
High-class Middle Eastern fare.

Moghul

Mena House Oberoi,
Pyramids Road, Gîza
Tel. 383 3222
Considered by many to be the best Indian restaurant in town, with refined moghul cuisine. Authentic Indian entertainment. Formal.

Naniwa

Ramses Hilton,
1115 Corniche El-Nil, Maspero
Tel. 744 400
Japanese fare with local gourmets.

Nubian Village

Le Méridien Hotel,
Corniche El-Nil, Garden City
Tel. 362 1717
Excellent Egyptian dishes in a delightful open-air riverside setting.

Paprika

1129 Corniche El-Nil
Tel. 749 447
Riverfront restaurant, popular with showbiz stars. European or Egyptian cuisine, especially mezzeh.

Peking

14 Saraya El-Ezbekiya Street
Tel. 349, 9086
Chinese fare in the town centre.

Prestige

43 Gezirat El-Arab Street,
Mohandessin
Tel. 347 0383
Italian restaurant renowned for its veal dishes. Pizza and pasta also.

Roy's

Cairo Marriott Hotel, Saraya
El-Gezira Street, Zamalek
Tel. 340 8888
Tex-Mex comes to Cairo.

Sakura ▯▯▯
5 Wissa Wassef,
Riyadh Tower, Gîza
Tel. 737 592
Japanese grills and other specialities served in style.

Tandoori ▯▯
11 Shehab Street, Mohandessin
Tel. 348 6301
Good north Indian fare, including tandoori 'barbecue' and vegetarian, in clean and simple surroundings. No alcohol.

Tarboush ▯▯▯
Heliopolis Sheraton, Oruba
Street, Heliopolis
Tel. 290 2027
Excellent lamb, quail and duck specialities served in traditional Egyptian style.

Tia Maria ▯
32 Jeddah Street, Mohandessin
Tel. 713 273
Simple Italian pasta and pizza at a bargain price.

Zanouba ▯▯
Atlas Zamalek Hotel, 20 Gamaet
El Dowal Al Arabia Street,
Mohandessin
Tel. 346 4175
A wide variety of robust Egyptian and Middle Eastern cooking in a simple style.

ALEXANDRIA AND THE MEDITERRANEAN

Andrea ▯
Agami Beach, Sharia El-Asal
Tel. 433 3227
Egyptian and Greek dishes.

Chez Gaby ▯
Foad Street (next to Royal
Cinema), Alexandria
Tel. 484 4300
Italian pasta and pizza, and Greek specialities.

Chicken Tikka ▯
Montazah Gardens, Alexandria
Tel. 547 5438
Indian and Egyptian cuisine.

Dynasty ▯▯
Ramada Renaissance Hotel, 544
El-Gueish Street, Alexandria
Tel. 866 111
Chinese cuisine, dinner only.

Hossny ▯
30 Safar Basha Street, Alexandria
Tel. 812 350
Egyptian and Middle Eastern fare. No alcohol.

Ismailiya Ashur ▯
Makne Street, Alexandria
Tel. 228 718
Traditional Egyptian cuisine, good lamb dishes.

77

Kadoura

74 July 26th Street, Alexandria
Tel. 800 967
Seafood Egyptian style.

Lord's Inn

12 Mohammed Ahmed Al Alili Street, Alexandria
Tel. 586 5664
High-class German cooking.

La Mamma

Montazah Sheraton Hotel, Corniche Road, Alexandria
Tel. 548 0550
Fine pizzas and various other Italian dishes.

Omar El-Khayam

200 July 26th Street, Alexandria
Tel. 483 3665
Good, simple Egyptian cuisine in plain surroundings.

Le Plat d'Or

Pullman Cecil Hotel, 16 Saad Zaghloul Square, Alexandria
Tel. 807 055
French and Italian cuisine in old-fashioned décor.

Rang Mahal

Pullman Cecil Hotel, 16 Saad Zaghloul Square, Alexandria
Tel. 807 055
Reputed to serve the best Indian food in Alexandria.

Samakmak

42 Kasr Ras El-Tin, Anfushi
Tel. 811 560
Very good grilled seafood.

San Giovanni

San Giovanni Hotel, 205 El-Gueish Street, Stanley, Alexandria
Tel. 546 7773
Landmark French restaurant overlooking the Mediterranean.

Santa Lucia

40 Safia Zaghloul, Alexandria
Tel. 482 0332
European cuisine in elegant décor.

Taverna Al Ramel

1 Saad Zaghloul Square, El-Ramleh, Alexandria
Tel. 482 8189
Greek and Egyptian cuisine.

Zephyrion

Aboukir
Tel. 546 2016
Seafront restaurant renowned for Egypt's best fresh seafood.

LUXOR

Class Restaurant

Class Shopping Centre, Khaled Ibn El-Walid Street
Tel. 376 327
Pleasant family restaurant serving Egyptian and European cuisine.

Club Med ▯▯▯
Club Méditerranée,
Khaled Ibn El-Walid Street
Tel. 580 850
Copious European buffet at lunch; à la carte menu for dinner.

El-Dawar ▯▯
Isis Hotel,
Khaled Ibn El-Walid Street
Tel. 373 3366
Good, rustic, Egyptian fare served amid country guest-house décor.

El-Karnak ▯▯▯
Luxor Sheraton,
El-Awameya Road
Tel. 374 544
All-day international cuisine with à la carte, speciality buffet menu which changes daily but includes a variety of Russian, Egyptian, and seafood dishes.

Jolie Ville ▯▯▯
Mövenpick Jolie Ville,
Crocodile Island
Tel. 374 855
First-class European buffet with daily specialities.

Khan El-Khalili ▯▯
Isis Hotel,
Khaled Ibn El-Walid Street
Tel. 373 3366
Good range of Egyptian and other Middle Eastern dishes.

La Mamma ▯▯
Luxor Sheraton,
El-Awameya Road
Tel. 374 544
Italian cuisine, complete with the accompaniment of live accordion entertainment.

Mövenpick ▯▯▯
Mövenpick Jolie Ville,
Crocodile Island
Tel. 374 855
Swiss cooking in a genteel atmosphere. Open for dinner only.

Palm Restaurant ▯▯▯
Luxor Hilton, New Karnak
Tel. 374 933
Egyptian and European cuisine, both buffet and à la carte.

La Terrazza ▯▯
Isis Hotel,
Khaled Ibn El-Walid Street
Tel. 373 3366
Italian restaurant serving hearty home-made pasta and pizza to hungry regulars.

White Corner ▯▯
Isis Hotel,
Khaled Ibn El-Walid Street
Tel. 373 3366
An excellent seafood restaurant from where clients enjoy magnificent views across the Nile to the Valley of the Kings.

79

ASWÂN

Le Club 1902 ▥▥▥
Pullman Cataract Hotel,
Abtal El-Tahrir Street, Aswân
Tel. 316 002
European and Egyptian cuisine in
a grand Moorish dining room.

Darna ▥▥▥▥
New Cataract Hotel,
Abtal El-Tahrir Street, Aswân
Tel. 323 434
Southern Egyptian cuisine in Nu-
bian surroundings. Open for din-
ner only.

El-Nashwa ▥▥▥
Aswân Oberoi, Elephantine Island
Tel. 323 455
Egyptian and European cuisine,
accompanied by nightclub enter-
tainment.

La Trattoria ▥▥
Isis Aswân Hotel,
Corniche El-Nil
Tel. 315 200
Home-made pasta and pizza.

RED SEA

Arlene's ▥▥
Dr Saâd Korayem Street,
Hurghada
American-run Tex-Mex, including
steaks and seafood.

Dolphin ▥▥
Magawish Tourist Village,
Hurghada
Tel. 442 620
Waterfront seafood restaurant.

Sheraton Seafood Restaurant ▥▥▥
Sheraton Hurghada Hotel,
Hurghada
Tel. 442 000
Spiny lobster and other delicacies.

SINAI

Casa Taba ▥▥▥
Taba Hilton, Taba
Tel. 763 544
Italian cuisine and elegant décor.

Fairouz Fish Restaurant ▥▥▥
Hilton Fairouz Village,
Na'ama Bay, Sharm El-Sheikh
Tel. 770 501
Beachfront seafood restaurant.

Marhaba ▥▥▥
Taba Hilton, Taba
Tel. 763 544
Good Middle Eastern cuisine.

Salah El-Deen ▥▥
Salah El-Deen Hotel, Taba
Tel. 771 345
Excellent seafood restaurant on
the beachfront.

Walking up the crunching gravel to the Rest-House, the **tomb of Tutankhamun** (No. 62) lies right in front of you. The tomb is very modest – the king died unexpectedly and was buried in a hurry – but is the only one ever discovered intact. The dazzling wealth of this single lesser king leaves the mind well and truly boggled when imagining the total extent of riches once secreted in this mystic valley.

Sacred apes glower from the walls, while four maidens are carved in Tutankhamun's sarcophagus to protect him. The gilded mummy-case in the sarcophagus contains the king's

Hieroglyphs

By the time Upper and Lower Egypt were united in 3000 BC, ancient Egyptians had devised their own alphabet: 24 simple-to-use pictorial letters. However, temple priests and scribes soon created a complex problem when they filled the hieroglyphic alphabet with some 700 signs and arcane symbols which only they could understand. The use of hieroglyphs died out at the end of the 4th century AD, though the ancient Egyptian language continued to be spoken by Copts.

The art of reading hieroglyphic inscriptions remained a mystery until Napoleon's soldiers found the three-language Rosetta Stone in 1799. With the help of the Stone, Jean-François Champollion, a French scholar, cracked the hieroglyphic code and discovered that hieroglyphs can be written right-to-left, left-to-right, or up-and-down. You can tell which way because the animals always look toward the beginning of the sentence. Kings and queens enclosed their names in 'cartouches':

Cleopatra   Ptolemy

mortal remains. The solid gold inner coffin has been removed to Cairo's Egyptian Museum (see p.33), along with the other treasures from the tomb.

Over 60 royal tombs have been uncovered so far in the Valley of the Kings, of which a dozen are usually open to the public. Repairs and preservations and restoration work is ongoing, however, so don't be surprised if one or more tombs are closed temporarily.

One of the most splendid is the **tomb of Seti I**, No. 17, south of the Rest-House. In the descending rooms and corridors, the murals have somehow kept their striking beauty and freshness for over 3,000 years. The lowest room once held the king's massive, alabaster sarcophagus (which is now in the John Soane Museum in London). The room's semi-cylindrical vault is painted as a blue sky with gods, goddesses and animals among the starry constellations. Wall paintings and excavation work in the lowest chambers show that the tomb was unfinished when Seti died.

Back down the path from Seti's tomb, keep to the left to reach the **tomb of Ramses III** (No. 11), with a fine, yellow-gold solar disc over the doorway. Inside, a corridor with small side-chambers bears interesting scenes of crafts and daily labours. In one scene, two harpists sing the praises of Ramses III before the gods.

Just a few steps west is the **tomb of Horemheb** (No. 57). The paintings here are notable for the heightened dramatic effect of their dark background. In the last room, the artists had hardly completed the preliminary sketches in red when Horemheb died.

Follow the right-hand path from here to reach the **tomb of Amenophis II** (No. 35), where the paintings, although plain with subdued colour, are finely executed. The richly decorated, sandstone sarcophagus of the king is still in place.

Workers resting in the Valley of the Kings, where ancestors carved tombs out of the rocks.

The **tomb of Thutmosis III** (No. 34) is worth the slight climb and scramble. It is the furthest south from the Rest-House, along a narrow path and up a steel stairway. Its decoration is plain and colour is used only sparingly, but the result is still very attractive.

After the hot and dusty but impressive tramp around the tombs, cool off with a much needed drink at the breezy terrace of the Rest-House.

FROM LUXOR TO ASWÂN

Upriver, stop at **Esna** (60km/ 37 miles south of Luxor) for the **Temple of Khnum**, divine creator, who moulded men and animals from Nile clay. Intriguingly, over the centuries, layers of civilization have raised the surrounding street level by 9m (30ft) around the temple. The surviving hypostyle hall was remodelled by the Ptolemies and Romans from a temple first built in the 18th Dynasty. Although harmonious in proportion, it is less refined than earlier Egyptian decorative art.

The town of **Edfu** (midway between Luxor and Aswân) boasts Egypt's best-preserved temple. Dedicated to Horus, the god of sun and planets, the falcon (his symbol) is a prominent decoration. It was one of the last Ptolemaic temples, finished only a few decades before the rise of Antony and Cleopatra. A horse-drawn carriage (*hantour*) offers one a delightful, if bone-rattling, five-minute ride from the Nile to the temple grounds.

Started in 237 bc by Ptolemy, the **Temple of Horus** has a pylon which is almost as huge as Karnak's (see p.56). The court is surrounded by 38 columns, and a granite statue of Horus stands guard at the entry to the first hypostyle hall. Columns and walls are covered in hieroglyphs detailing offerings to the god. At the centre of the holy of holies is a huge granite monolith, hollowed out as a sanctuary, with another block in front for bearing the sacred barque, a modern replica of which can be seen in the room behind. Unlike other temples which are bathed in brilliant sunlight because they have have lost their roofs, the Edfu temple preserves the gloom of surrounding chambers, lit only by tiny windows in the stone.

Further up the river, **Kom Ombo Temple** is exquisitely situated on a dune above a bend in the Nile. Alone among Egypt's temples, it is shared equally by two gods: Sobek, the crocodile god of Nile fertility, and Haroeris, the elder Horus, symbolized by falcon head and solar disc. Although the first temple dates back to the 18th Dynasty, almost all that remains is Ptolemaic, and dates from around 300 BC.

In order to avoid resentment between the two gods, everything here is in pairs: double doorways lead into the great court and then through two hypostyle halls to a double sanctuary. Situated to the right of the temple entrance is a small chapel dedicated to Hathor but now housing Sobek's mummified crocodiles. North of the temple court, a stone staircase descends to the local Nilometre at the bottom of a well.

ASWÂN

The town of Aswân (population 200,000) was invaded in the 1960s by a flood of 2,000 engineers from the (then) Soviet Union, directing 35,000 Egyptian construction workers in the building of a giant dam across the Nile. The electricity and flood control facilities of the Aswân High Dam (Sad el-Aali) were responsible for profound changes to the economy and agriculture of Egypt. Despite some unforeseen ecological problems, most agree that the benefits of the project more than compensate for the drawbacks. Completed in 1972, the dam completely changed the town's character and provides a third of Egypt's electricity.

Once a town of peasants, holiday-makers and archaeologists not that different from Luxor, Aswân fast became an industrial centre with iron and steel factories, and plants for fertilizer chemicals and sugar. In spite of these changes, the centre of town remains pleasantly easy-going, particularly around the bazaar, while the **85**

Ready to carry visitors back to Aswân, feluccas wait by the jetty at Elephantine Island.

surroundings also retain much of the charm that made this a favourite wintering spot for the late Aga Khan and a number of other wealthy visitors.

White-sailed *feluccas* glide up and down the Nile among the islands like tall, graceful waterbirds. It's worth getting up at dawn to catch the gold and grey of the desert hills, the twitter of birds, and the braying donkeys in nearby farms. At the hotels and cruise-docks, horse-drawn carriages (*hantours*) wait to take you for a ride among the eucalyptus, citrus and palm trees.

Take a taxi from the centre of town to the **Aswân High Dam** (about 10km/6 miles). For a fine view of the dam and Lake Nasser, ride to the top of the lotus-shaped monument, dedicated to Russian-Egyptian co-operation. The lake stretches over 500km (312 miles) to the south, across the Egyptian frontier into Sudan.

Industry of a different sort brought wealth to Aswân in pharaonic times. The beautiful red granite of Egypt's colossal sculptures and major monuments was taken from local quarries, a few minutes' ride by car from the centre of town. A massive unfinished obelisk, measuring 27m (90ft) long,

fractured during cutting and abandoned, shows how these magnificent monuments were painstakingly hewn by hand and then polished to a glassy smoothness.

Hire a *felucca* for a tour of the west bank of the Nile and the islands. **Elephantine Island**, the largest, is home to the ruined Temple of Khnum, the work of many pharaohs down to the Ptolemies and the Romans. The Aswân Museum, housed in an early 20th-century villa, is right next to the ruins. Stairs cut into the rock below the villa drop down to the Aswân Nilometre, which still has its elegant water-level markers made out of marble. **Kitchener's Island** (or Botanic Island or Island of Flowers) was a gift to Britain's Consul-General – a subsequent war-hero and lover of flowers. Now a botanical garden, it offers a pleasant stroll in the cool of the day. At the island's southern tip is a duck research station – just follow the quacks.

Up above the west bank of the Nile is the **Mausoleum of the Aga Khan** – his full title, **87**

Philae's Temple of Isis celebrates the most enduringly popular of Egyptian goddesses.

Sultan Muhammad Shah Al-Huseini, Aga Khan III, 48th Imam of the Shia Imami Ismailis, was something of a mouthful. (The latter form a Moslem sect living chiefly in Iran and Pakistan.) The Aga Khan (1877-1957) built a hillside villa in Aswân, fell in love with the area, and decided to stay forever.

From the mausoleum, it's a 20-minute mule- or camel-ride along a winding, desert path to the ruined 7th-century **Coptic Monastery of St Simeon**.

To the north along the west bank of the Nile lies a typical Nubian village with its easy-paced life mostly unchanged through the centuries. Ducks, donkeys and goats amble in the streets, young girls fetch buckets of water from a canal, and, one of the few signs of modernity, groups of boys escape work in the fields for a hectic game of football.

Carved in the hillside above are rock tombs of local potentates known as the Lords of Elephantine Island. Some interesting traces of decoration survive, as do both pigeons and bats. A few tombs contain stone sacrificial altar-blocks, and the 12th Dynasty **tomb of Sarambot I** (or Sirenput), still has his wife's mummy greeting you in the shadows with eyeless sockets. These tombs, among the oldest in Egypt, are also worth visiting for the fine view of Aswân and the Nile from their hillside ledge.

TEMPLES OF PHILAE

When many of Aswân's great pharaonic temples were threatened by the rising waters of Lake Nasser during construction of the High Dam, the most important were transferred to higher ground. The temples on Philae Island were one of the most impressive sights in the country, but even they were partially submerged behind the Old Dam (completed around 1900). Once decided, the High Dam operations threatened to wipe them out totally. In a vast international rescue effort coordinated by UNESCO, they were painstakingly reassembled in all their glory on the island of Agilkia, some 300m (980ft) to the north.

The **Great Temple of Isis**, which flourished about Jesus' time, is the largest and most distinctive island temple. This, the **mammisi** (birth-temple – honouring the child Horus) and the **Temple of Hathor** (the sky goddess) form the setting for one of Egypt's most spectacular nightly sound-and-light shows.

KALABSHA

On Lake Nasser's west shore, 1km (0.5 miles) south of the Aswân High Dam, accessible by taxi then boat, the **temples of Kalabsha** have also been heroically relocated from their now flooded site 50km (30 miles) further south. The classic Egyptian **Temple of Mandoulis**, built in Roman times, is the largest. To the left of the entrance is the pretty little **Temple of Kertassi**, the capitals of which bear Hathor's half-human, half-bovine face. Behind the Temple of Mandoulis is **Beit El-Wali**, with murals depicting the military campaigns of Ramses II.

ABU SIMBEL

Of Egypt's many thrills, from a first glimpse of the pyramids (see p.37) to a quiet moment in Karnak's great hypostyle hall (see p.56), few are more moving than the confrontation with the four huge statues of Ramses II at Abu Simbel. It is worth an overnight stay at one of the small hotels here so as **89**

to rise at daybreak and watch the sun illuminate the temple façade, penetrating the depths of its inner sanctum. Failing that, take a pre-dawn trip from Aswân to appreciate the grandeur of the Western Desert.

Here, at the limits of Upper Egypt, Ramses II built his temple to Amon-Ra (Sun God), Ptah (God of Creativity), Har-

Nowhere is the personality cult more stupendous than in Abu Simbel's statues of Ramses II.

makhis (Guardian of the Gates to the Nether World), and, of course, himself. The **four colossal figures** are each 20m (65ft) high, directly face the rising sun and are all of the pharaoh himself, with queen and daughters in miniature at his feet. Above the entrance is the high-relief figure of Amon-Ra. A row of baboons, symbols of wisdom, sit along the upper border of the tall façade.

Inside the temple are more gigantic statues of Ramses II, but now in the guise of Osiris. Bas-reliefs depict offerings to

the gods, military gains, and the merciless treatment of captives. At the temple's heart, Ramses II sits in state with the gods to whom the construction is dedicated.

The perfection of Ramses' accomplishment is echoed in restoration work carried out by UNESCO in conjunction with a Swedish firm from 1968 to 1972. A doorway to the right of the façade leads inside the artificial mountain made to receive the temple. Charts and diagrams tell of the temple's move from a spot now submerged by Lake Nasser to its new man-made site, air-conditioned inside.

The caretaker, bearing the giant *ankh* (life symbol) temple key of magnificent proportions, lets you into the smaller **Temple of Hathor**. Four statues on the façade are of Ramses II, with two of his queen, Nefertari, dressed as Hathor. The decoration inside favours the feminine side of the Egyptian pantheon, although Ramses II cannot stay away. The benevolent cow at the heart of the temple is Hathor.

The Western Oases

For a real sense of the Egypt beyond the Nile, there is no more exhilarating a trip than a tour of the Western Desert oases. After a surfeit of mobs and museums, enjoy a prolonged moment of contemplation in the wilderness, with the fabulous constellations of the sky at night, and the miracle of the lush green oases. Foreign conquerors tried to penetrate the desert's mysteries, with some, like the Persian Cambyses in 525 BC, losing whole armies in the process. These days four-wheel-drive vehicles will get you out safely.

You can fly or drive to **El-Khârga**, due west of Luxor, the administrative capital of the region known now as New Valley. This is a fully-fledged town of some 50,000 inhabitants, which serves as a springboard for desert tours. Out in the dunes, beyond the treeline of the El-Khârga Oasis to the north, is the ancient Christian cemetery of **Bagawat**, a splendid collection of monumental **91**

SUEZ, SINAI AND THE RED SEA

MEDITERRANEAN SEA

ISRAEL

Gaza

Rafah

Beersheba

Port Said

El-Arish

✈ ALEXANDRIA

Damanhûr

Pelusium

Suez Canal

El-Alamein →

Zagazig

Ismailiya

Wadi el-Natrûn

NEGEV

Wadi el-Arish

Gîza

✈ CAIRO

Ahmed Hamdi Tunnel

Suez

Port Tawfik

Nakhl

Birket Qârûn

Springs of Moses

Fayyoum

Sudr

Râs el Sudr

Eilat

Taba

Aqaba

Pharaoh's Island

Hamman Pharaun (Pharaoh's Baths)

JORDAN

Nuweiba

Abu Rudeis

SINAI

Wadi Faran

River Nile

Wadi Sannûr

St. Catherine's ✈ Monastery

SAUDI ARAB

Wadi el-Tarfa

St. Catherine ▲ Mt. Catherine (2,642m/8,668ft)

Dahab

▲ Mt. Sinai (2,285m/7,497ft)

Minya

EGYPT

El-Tûr

Gulf of Suez

EASTERN DESERT

✈ Sharm El-Sheikh

Râs Mohammed

WESTERN DESERT

✈ Assiut

RED SEA

River Nile

Sohâg

Wadi Qena

✈ Hurghada

Safâga

Farâfra, Dakhla Oasis, Balat →

El-Khârga

✈ Qena

El-Khârga Oasis

✈ Luxor

Esna

Aswân, Lake Nasser →

Edfu

✈	Airport
〰	Motorway
═	Main Road
	Marshland
	Land below 200m
	Land above 200m
	Land above 1000m

0 _____ 160 k

0 _____ 100 m

tombs dating back to the 5th and 6th centuries. Down in a hollow are the remains of the fortified **monastery of Mustapha Kashif**, which is named after the 11th-century Moslem governor who appropriated it as an office for tax collecting. Closer to town is the **Temple of Hibis**, which was begun in 568 BC and completed under the Persian rule of Darius, but has subsequent Ptolemaic and Roman additions.

The road from El-Khârga west to the **Dakhla oasis** takes you past fascinating rock formations. Many in the shape of sphinxes or camels have prehistoric inscriptions, and it is not clear whether the 'sculptures' themselves were fashioned by the hand of man or by desert sandstorms. East of the main town, off the El-Khârga road, is the charming little village of **Balat**, with its narrow, sheltered streets, where it is necessary to duck through tunnels to get from one house to another. Hospitable elders may invite you to share their mint tea beneath the shade of the courtyard figtree as they study the Koran. In Dakhla's main town, **Mut**, there is a small museum which displays local craftwork.

Dakhla's situation, right in the midst of the burning desert, means that its great joy is its cool green **gardens**, shady olive groves, and orchards of mangoes, apricots, apples and mandarines, which are irrigated by gushing streams. Further north, the small village of **Farâfra** has wide open streets with mudbrick wells, and is also surrounded by its share of delightful shady gardens and orchards abounding in guavas, oranges and apricots.

The grand attraction in this area is a camel or jeep safari out into the magical wilderness of the **White Desert**, to the north east of the village. Monoliths in the most fantastic shapes of monstrous animals and giant humans stand amidst endless stretches of powdered white chalk 'sand'. Take warm clothes and plenty of blankets if you come to spend a night out there, and enjoy the experience of the sunset, the starry night and the dawn.

93

The Red Sea

Many people suffering from an overdose of pyramids and temples in the Nile Valley relax body and soul with a less exhausting form of sun-worship along 1,600km (1,000 miles) of Red Sea coastline.

The resort of **Hurghada** is developing rapidly, with direct flights from Cairo or Luxor, or a bearable coach-ride across the Eastern Desert from Qena. It offers first-rate hotel facilities and holiday villages with endless stretches of fine, white sand. The **watersports** are excellent, including snorkelling and deep-sea fishing. In town, the **bazaar** offers a good array of Bedouin and other folk art, and the **aquarium** shows the exotic tropical fish you can expect to see swimming in the coral. (Remember when scuba diving or snorkelling: look but don't touch.)

Safâga, further along the coast, was once a commercial port but is now also opening as a holiday-village resort. Both seafood and watersport facilities are good.

The Suez Canal and the Sinai

Since the peace treaty with Israel, the Suez Canal and the Sinai desert have opened up again to tourism to offer a diversity of attractions, from the spirituality of Mount Sinai and St Catherine's Monastery to the relaxation of the beaches at Sharm El-Sheikh and Taba. You can fly directly to Sharm El-Sheikh or drive from Cairo via the Suez Canal. Cruise liners stop off at the northern end of the canal at Port Said.

PORT SAID

Founded in the 19th century at the time of the construction of the Suez Canal, **Port Said** was known in Victorian times as the Gateway to the East, and was popular amongst passengers stopping off on cruises. Today it is a key link between the Mediterranean and the Red Sea, bringing the trade of Asia to Africa. As such, it has come under repeated bombardment in time of war, but has been rebuilt and thrives now as a lively free zone. The Egyptians exercise ancient trading talents from the souk, offering electronic exotica from Japan, Korea and Singapore.

Take a harbour cruise to see the ocean-going vessels being slowly piloted into the canal. The **Port Said National Museum** has a major collection of 10,000 art pieces, which range from pre-Dynastic and Pharaonic, to Greco-Roman, Coptic and Islamic.

The Suez Canal

Ever since the time of the pharaohs, men have been planning a canal linking the Mediterranean and the Red Sea, either via the Nile or through the isthmus east of the delta. Indeed, from carvings we know there was a canal joining the Nile and the Red Sea during Seti I's reign from 1312–1290 BC.

Around 600 BC, Necho II abandoned work on a canal from the Nile to the Red Sea after oracles warned the work would only serve the trade interests of foreign invaders. A century later the Persian ruler, Darius, dug a canal roughly along the bed of the present one from Ismailiya to Cairo. It silted up and was restored by Roman Emperor Trajan around AD 100 but had disintegrated again by the time of the 8th-century *caliphs*.

Napoleon's engineers created a channel along the canal's present bed, but abandoned it after mistakenly calculating that the Red Sea was 10m (32ft) higher than the Mediterranean, necessitating a costly system of locks. Ferdinand de Lesseps, French consul in Cairo, persuaded Khedive Said Pacha to revive the project, and in 1869, ten years after work began, the Suez Canal was completed. A grand imperialist effort, it was opened by France's Empress Eugénie, and inaugurated in the presence of French, Austrian and Russian Royalty, with Britain getting involved six years later. In 1956, President Nasser's nationalization of the canal resulted in the war of Suez.

The canal was closed during further fighting in 1973 and reopened in 1975 by President Sadat after turmoils had ceased.

A desert oasis (right) holds more appeal for these Bedouins than a lone acacia in the Sinai.

ISMAILIYA

Midway down the Suez Canal, around 120km (75 miles) on a direct highway north east of Cairo, **Ismailiya** (named after the Khedive Ismail, governor of Egypt) has a faded colonial charm amidst green parks on **Lake Timsah**'s western shore. **96** The lake offers good sailing and windsurfing, as well as handsome beaches. Take a late afternoon promenade on the **Mohammed Ali Quay**. The local museum houses the private collection of Ferdinand de Lesseps, who built the Suez Canal, and gives pride of place to the granite stele (column) erected by Darius, the ancient Persian whose canal linked the Red Sea to the Nile.

SUEZ CITY

Badly damaged in successive Arab-Israeli wars, the town of **Suez City** has been attractively rebuilt with plenty of greenery and good beaches on Suez Bay. Flags from all over the world flutter over the harbour, and in summer the city hosts a colourful parade of pilgrims *en route* to Mecca.

Port Tawfik, around 1.5km (1 mile) south and on the other side of the canal, is the place to watch the great freighters coming in and out of the canal. On a promontory overlooking the mouth of the canal stands an eloquently empty pedestal – meant for the statue of Ferdinand de Lesseps, but removed following the abortive invasion of Suez by his fellow Frenchmen in 1956.

SINAI WEST COAST

Access by road to the west coast of the Sinai peninsula is through the **Ahmed Hamdi Tunnel**, 12km (7 miles) north of Suez City and named after an Egyptian hero of the 1973 war against Israel. The debris of tanks and aircraft from that and previous Sinai campaigns can still be seen from the coast road as you drive south.

This is the route that Moses is believed to have taken when leading his followers on their Exodus from Egypt. Tradition says that **Uyun Musa** (Springs of Moses), 45km (28 miles) south of the tunnel, is the spot where Moses found drinking water for the parched Israelites. It is now a rather sorry-looking well surrounded by a few palm trees and Bedouins selling trinkets.

A further 80km (50 miles) south is **Hammam Pharaun** (Pharaoh's Baths), a hot spring which comes from deep inside a hillside cave to spill out onto the sandy beach. At 72°C (161°F) it's plenty hot enough to boil an egg. **97**

ST CATHERINE'S MONASTERY AND MOUNT SINAI

There are flights to St Catherine's small airport, but the best route is by road from the west, then east from the Abu Rudeis oil-fields, through landscapes of purple, gold and vermilion-coloured mountains, closing in on the **Wadi Faran oasis** of green acacias and cascades of date palms. Around the monastery itself, the accommodation runs from luxury chalets to simple but good campsites.

St Catherine's stands high (1,570m/5,150ft) at the head of a valley, beneath the mountain where it is believed Moses received the Ten Commandments. At the Greek Orthodox **Monastery**, which was founded by Emperor Justinian in AD 527, part of the original masonry is still visible in the huge walls of that genuine fortress, complete with battlements.

The 10th-century **mosque** near the entrance of the monastery church was imposed by the Sultan for equality. The Byzantine church has a rich collection of **icons** and **mosaics** in the narthex, as well as a triple-naved basilica. With barely a dozen monks left to run the establishment, it is difficult to get authorization to visit the precious library and monastic treasure; but see the **garden** with its cypresses and fruit trees. Also popular is the somewhat ghoulish **ossuary** of monks' skulls and bones (only skeletons of archbishops are kept intact), including the 6th-century St Stephen, still wearing his monk's habit.

Controversy continues over whether **Mount Sinai** is Gebel Musa (Mount Moses, 2,285m/ 7,497ft), its taller sister, Gebel Katherina (Mount Catherine, 2,642m/8,668ft) – both nearby – or another Sinai mountain altogether. At any rate, the pre-dawn climb can be an almost spiritual experience (if you get up before the crowds gather on the slopes). Dress warmly for the bitter desert cold – take a flask of hot tea or coffee – and you may want to pay extra to a Bedouin to lead you up the lower slopes by camel. You won't forget the Sinai sunrise.

SHARM EL-SHEIKH

Biblical scholars believe this to be Ophira, from where King Solomon transported the gold for his throne. More recently, scuba divers insist that this southern tip of the Sinai peninsula is one of the world's best locations for deep-sea diving. Even inexperienced swimmers can appreciate the wonders of Red Sea coral and fish, with training at hotels equipped for every kind of watersport. Non-swimmers can take a glass-bottomed boat. As well as superb sandy beaches, the resort has a magnificent backdrop of mountains – perfect at sunset.

Also on the coast, try the ultimate underwater adventure in **Râs Mohammed National Park**'s protected creeks (don't forget: look, but don't touch!).

EAST COAST RESORTS

North along the Sinai's east coast are several new resorts, notably **Dahab**, **Nuweiba** and **Taba** (on the Israeli border), the last having the best hotels (see p.72). In the bay south of

Taba is picturesque **Pharaoh's Island**, where you can visit the great sultan Saladin's reconstructed 12th-century fortress.

St Catherine's Monastery, at the foot of Mount Sinai, where the Jews received their Law.

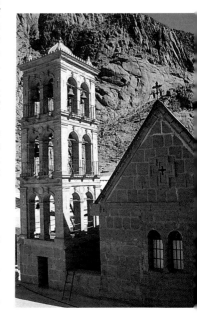

What to Do

Shopping

The **Khan El-Khalili** bazaar in Cairo is world famous for its wealth of shopping opportunities. Antique or modern, simple or elegant, some handicraft item will inevitably draw your eye. It is customary to haggle, and you will invariably be rewarded for your efforts by a truly remarkable change in price. If you take a guide or interpreter, remember it is standard practice for him to get some of the money spent on every purchase. Sometimes, a detour to a back-street or rooftop workshop will give you the chance to buy at reduced rates.

Here are some of Egypt's best buys, which are available in Khan El-Khalili and also in tourist shops and bazaars in other Egyptian cities:

Alabaster: the word itself is said to derive from the name of an Egyptian town. Shops sell flower vases, decorative boxes, statuettes and other ornaments. The stone comes from the Nile Valley and is worked, among other places, in Luxor.

Antiquities: although licensed dealers could once sell genuine antique pieces of jewellery and artefacts, this trade is no longer legal. If you are caught transporting antiquities the penalties are stiff. Fakes abound – your best bet is often a good-quality copy from the shops of the major museums.

Copper and Brass: the tinkling of a coppersmith's hammers is a familiar sound in Khan El-Khalili. It takes about a day and a half to chisel the arabesques into a small copper tray. The best trays, samovars, coffee sets and other items are generally the older ones, but new copper and brass is often cheaper, and still attractive.

Cotton goods: Egyptian cotton's long fibres and smooth finish make it among the highest grades in the world – good news for T-shirts. Mohammed Ali built his dynasty's wealth on cotton. Many European tailors will stitch up shirts to order in a few days, or you can choose from ready-made ones. *Gallabiyas*, the long and loose Egyptian outer garments, are comfortable, attractive and are worn by both men and women. Look at several sizes and qualities of cloth: unpolished cotton is cheaper than the more chic, polished variety.

Jewellery: gold and silver are normally sold by weight, with a small mark-up for detailed workmanship. Take your pick from pharaonic styles inspired by King Tutankhamun's treasure, arabesques or more modern pieces. Semi-precious and precious stones are also sold by weight at attractive prices, whether set in a piece of jewellery or not. Shop around before buying.

Leather goods: if you bargain well, handbags, shoulder bags and satchels are all good buys, but do inspect each piece very carefully for flaws and careless workmanship. Some shops sell camel saddles, which make an

Long fibres and a smooth finish: the quality of Egyptian cotton is among the finest in the world.

unusual purchase and are hard to find outside Egypt, although before buying you should ask yourself: where am I going to buy a camel?

Tapestries: the children of El-Harraniye (a village on the road to Saqqara) produce eye- **101**

catching designs that can brighten up any wall or enliven any table-top. They are made in different shapes and sizes – although colours and motifs will probably be the basis of your criteria when choosing.

The choice at Khan El-Khalili market is endless... the only problem is how to get it home.

Genuine Harraniye tapestries tend to be rather expensive, but cheaper imitations and copies – albeit of a widely varying quality – can also be found.

Woodwork: some of the most attractive woodwork you are ever likely to see comes from Egypt. Foremost is *mashra-biyya*, lathe-turned screens of intricate wooden lattice work, which covered Egyptian windows in the old days, shielding women from what their husbands and fathers feared as the curious stares of strange men.

Screens, room-dividers and tray-stands are sold at reasonable prices, but do think about the problems of transportation before you buy anything. An alternative choice, more easily packed, is a small box of cedar or sandalwood, which are usually inlaid with ivory, mother-of-pearl and ebony. Each tiny piece of inlay is manoeuvred into place with a pair of tweezers and glued by hand. If you do have luggage-space, consider one of the larger boxes, or an inlaid chessboard, or perhaps even a small table.

Folklore and Festivals

Festival time in Egypt finds everyone outdoors, following colourful street processions, strolling along the banks of the Nile, or filling the parks and gardens. Vendors sell snacks and refreshing drinks, and the crowds eagerly pay court to itinerant performers. Dancers, wrestlers and singers all put on open-air shows, cheerfully collecting coins at the end of each performance.

A favourite diversion is the mock-battle called **El-Tahtib**: two men armed with stout reed staffs walk in a circle facing each other, swinging the staffs above their heads. It looks like a courtly dance, but each combatant is tinglingly alert, waiting for the opportunity to take a swing at his opponent. A split-second of inattention by one player, and the heavy staff of the other speeds down, but there's time to parry, and the two weapons meet with a resounding thwack.

When players are equally-matched, El-Tahtib becomes a graceful ceremony of flowing movements and mutual respect. Let a wily old master take on a young and inexperienced hot-blood, however, and the blows come thick and fast. Strength and agility are less important than experience and reflexes, and the old man always comes out teaching the novice a few tricks.

The **Nubian folklore** and music of Upper Egypt is very different from the Arabic folklore of Cairo and the Nile Delta. Nubians have their own languages (though most speak Arabic as well), and traditional Nubian music sounds surprisingly Far Eastern in its tones and rhythms.

In the celebration of major **Islamic and traditional festivals**, all Egyptians are united. The National Spring Festival, **Sham En Nessim**, is celebrated on the Monday following Coptic Easter. It's an excuse for everyone to get outdoors or into boats on the Nile to pursue an old legend. 'He who sniffs the first spring zephyr', so the saying goes, 'will have good health all year'.

103

Another significant holiday is **Mulid En Nabi**, the Prophet's Birthday, when a mammoth procession winds its way through Cairo's streets, with smaller ones in other cities.

Ramadan is a period of 30 days, the ninth month of the Moslem lunar calendar. During this time, all good Moslems observe strict fasting between the hours of sunrise and sunset. The rules are stiff: starting at first light, no food or drink, no smoking or even licking a stamp. Working hours are also reduced.

At sunset, special dishes fill the feast tables for the evening breaking of the fast, the meal of *iftar*. Pregnant women, children, the infirm and travellers are exempted from the fast, and everyone else takes advantage of shorter working hours. Hotels and restaurants keep normal hours for their non-Moslem visitors, though many stop serving alcoholic drinks. At the end of the holy month is **Ramadan Bairam** (Eid El-Fitr), a three-day celebration marked with greeting-cards and visits to friends.

Perhaps the most sacred of Moslem festivals is the **Qurban Bairam** (Eid El-Adha), which is celebrated in the middle of the month of Zu'l-Hegga, when many Moslems undertake the *hajj*, or pilgrimage, to Mecca. The four-day feast commemorates the biblical sacrifice by Abraham, when a ram was substituted for his son at the last minute – Moslems relive the moment by sacrificing a ram. After the ritual slaughter according to Koranic law, the meat is cooked and a feast is prepared for family and friends, with a generous portion going to the poor.

August used to be a time of elaborate festivals in Cairo. As the waters of the Nile rose in the annual flood, **Nilometres** located along the river would be checked and rechecked, and the readings sent off to Cairo by messenger. When the water level reached a certain point, the canals would be unblocked and the precious water would surge deep into the fields, carrying valuable silt to replenish the soil. Now that the Aswân High Dam controls the Nile's flow at an even level all year round, the August festivities have only an echo of their former gaiety and importance.

The **Cairo Film Festival**, which was first held in 1977, has proved a great success and a major cultural event in the Middle East. It normally takes place in November, screening award-winning films from all over the world at some of the major hotels.

tennis court, a racetrack, golf course, squash and handball courts, swimming pools and every other imaginable sports facility. Due to demand, some clubs are very exclusive, with strict entrance criteria and a hefty annual fee. Clubs which welcome temporary members are: the Cairo Yacht Club, Heliopolis Sporting Club, Maadi Sporting Club, Maadi Yacht Club, Mena Golf Club, and the Shooting Club.

Sports

In Cairo and Alexandria there are many sports clubs which were once patronized only by wealthy foreigners and Egyptian nobility. Today things are more democratic, and tourists can take out either temporary or short-term memberships (details from your hotel).

In the heart of Cairo, on the island of Gezira, are dozens of

A sport of cheerful meditation: fishing in the sun along the Mediterranean coast.

Watersports: as long as you don't swim in the Nile, you can enjoy a lot of fun both in and on the water during your stay in Egypt. As well as the miles of beaches in Alexandria and along the Mediterranean coast (see p.42), amenities for swimming are offered by almost every large hotel (these are available to outsiders, but for a fee).

At the resorts of Hurghada and Port Safâga on the Red Sea (see p.94), the conditions are superb for **snorkelling** and **scuba diving**. In the Sinai, the best watersports facilities are available at Sharm El-Sheikh (see p.99) – in particular the deep sea diving at Râs Mohammed close by. Fierce new competition is also offered by the resorts of Dahab, Nuweiba and Taba (see p.99), which are situated up the coast of the Gulf of Aqaba.

The Red Sea offers perfect conditions for jet-skiing, with plenty of space for swimmers and skiers.

Fishing: at all Red Sea and Sinai resorts, there are boats for hire for deep-sea fishing. Many hotels will also provide a beach-barbecue on which to cook your catch.

Horse-riding: it doesn't matter whether you prefer sunlight or moonlight, you can hire a horse for an hour or a day, with a guide or without. Rates are reasonable, although you may have to do some haggling. One of the most exciting trails in the country runs from the stables at the pyramids of Gîza along the edge of the desert to the pyramids at Abusir and Saqqara. At Luxor, in the Valley of the Kings, you can tour tombs and temples by camel.

Entertainment

Sound-and-light Shows

The grandeur of the pyramids (see p.37) is enhanced at night by powerful floodlights which bathe the ancient stones in rich colour. A stirring commentary accompanied by music hails from concealed loudspeakers. Sound-and-light shows at the pyramids are given in English, French or German. Check performance times, as these vary with the time of year. You can take a taxi to the pyramids and pay the entry fee yourself, or join an all-inclusive bus tour.

In Luxor, the show is at Karnak's Great Temple of Amon (see p.56). Spectators follow light effects and a commentary through the temple, then sit in tiered seats behind the Sacred Lake. In Aswân, an enthralling spectacle dramatizes the Temples of Philae (see p.89).

Remember a sweater for the evening chill.

Cinemas

Check local English-language newspapers for film showings. You'll usually find something in English or with English subtitles. In cinemas here everyone has a reserved seat. Buy your tickets an hour or more in advance (especially on Thursday, Friday or Saturday night).

Clubs

Clubs in the large hotels stage nightly shows with both Western song-and-dance and fiery Egyptian music. As soon as your blood is racing, on comes the belly-dancer, with music **107** building to fever-pitch as she performs muscular impossibilities and sinuous gyrations. Dancing then follows. Though both exciting and entertaining, hotel shows are good, clean family fun.

Some hotel clubs and discothèques require membership or payment of a door charge to enter. Dance music comes from the latest records, but a belly-dancer and oriental band are often brought in to add to the quality of entertainment.

Pyramids Road in Cairo is lined with glittery nightspots, some of them quite racy. Visitors in search of more modest entertainment should stick to the city centre.

Opera

Cairo's Opera House was an official gift from the Japanese government in 1988. The complex, which also houses several art galleries, is on Gezira Island and is worth a visit. Foreign and Egyptian performances are held from October to May. Note that formal dress is required.

Casinos

Only foreigners are allowed into Egypt's gambling houses – gambling being an Islamic taboo. You should bring your passport, and only foreign currency may be used at tables. Most luxury hotels have casinos, with roulette, blackjack, baccara and, increasingly so, one-armed bandits.

If you see 'Casino' on a sign by a Nile-side restaurant, don't be fooled. In the Middle East, a casino can be any waterside establishment from a snack bar to a restaurant with floor show, but there will definitely *not* be any gambling.

National Circus

Egypt's National Circus was started with the help of Soviet circus masters some time ago and has been, along with the Aswân Dam, one of the more welcome legacies. Acrobats, clowns and animals perform in Cairo's Agouza Quarter during most of the year, moving to Alexandria for the hot months of July and August.

Eating Out

In a country with such a long history, it's intriguing to think that as a modern-day visitor to Egypt you might be eating much the same as the pharaohs did. Certainly many things are unchanged. You eat the same fish from the Mediterranean and Red Sea, and the Nile Valley and Delta yield the same sheep, cattle, pigeons, game, ducks, grain and vegetables that appear in the old wall paintings. More recent history has also had a culinary impact on Egyptian food, and Italian, Turkish, French and English influences are all to be found in Egyptian cookery. Present-day internationalism provides an additional touch, bringing everything from chow mein to Wiener Schnitzel, fried chicken to take-away hamburgers, and pizza to Indian curry.

A narguileh *water-pipe can be as important to a Cairo meal as an aperitif in a Paris bistro.*

*E*ven in the desert, a proper meal starts off with mezzeh and pitah bread.

In your hotel, the normal continental **breakfast** of coffee or tea, toast, rolls, butter and jam may be supplemented with fresh fruit juice and salty white or pale yellow cheese. Larger hotels lay on copious buffets of cooked American or Egyptian dishes.

Lunch is the main meal of the day, but many hotels cater to foreign habits and serve the big meal in the evening. From one o'clock until three or four in the afternoon is the usual lunchbreak, although Cairenes eat later than Westerners.

Dinner in Egyptian homes is also usually served late, perhaps not until 10pm. During Ramadan (see p.104) both the hours and much of the food served changes completely.

EGYPTIAN CUISINE

Many hotels serve more European dishes than Egyptian, but don't miss any chance to savour the local fare.

For an interesting sampling, many restaurants offer *mezzeh* – a selection of local salads, cheese, stuffed vine leaves and sometimes meat. An enjoyable first course amongst a group of friends, *mezzeh* can be a light meal in itself.

An alternative is *molokhia*, a savoury soup made from the green leafy vegetable which is cooked with garlic, pepper and coriander in broth, and usually eaten with rice and chicken. No Egyptian would do without *ful*, thick and tangy bean-stew flavoured with tomatoes and spices. It is commonly served with oil and fresh lime juice or with deep-fried *taamia*, a paste made of the same beans plus other vegetables, mixed with parsley and spices. *Makhallal* (*turshi*), spicy pickled vegetables, are an important accessory on Egyptian tables.

Bread: mostly the flat Middle Eastern *pitah* type, especially suited for scooping up *leben zabadi* (yogurt), *tahina* (sesame seed purée), or its variation, *baba ganoug* (*tahina* and a purée of baked aubergine /eggplant, lemon and garlic).

Meat: some restaurants specialize in *kebab*, juicy chunks of lamb or mutton marinated in spices and charcoal-grilled on a spit. A variation is *kofta*, spiced minced or ground lamb, wrapped on a flat skewer and grilled the same way, then served on a bed of fresh parsley or coriander leaf.

Game: Grilled or stuffed quail or pigeon from the Nile Delta, served with rice, is a favourite.

Fish: fresh from the Red Sea, Mediterranean or Lake Nasser, fish is usually pan- or deep-fried, sometimes spiced with a pinch of cumin during cooking. Large Alexandrian shrimp are a speciality, grilled on a skewer over a charcoal brazier.

Salads: served before and during the main course. Boiled cold beetroot is popular in season, as are the excellent, ripe sliced tomatoes and cucumbers, which are served with a dash of lemon juice or vinegar. Green salads may contain a tart, almost peppery green leaf called *gargir* with the lettuce.

Cheese: generally quite salty. Like those pickled vegetables, cheese may be good for water retention in a desert climate, but it's no treat for the taste buds. Imported cheese is widely available.

Fruit: try the Delta's fresh bananas, oranges, figs, mangoes, grapes or guavas. There are many varieties of **date**, most quite different from the sweet type back home.

Pastry-desserts: look for the many delicious varieties, most of Turkish origin and impossibly sweet, but let yourself go. A great local delicacy is *omali*, a baked dessert of pastry, milk, raisins and coconut. Its fans insist it is delicious even when made badly, and it is unquestionably heavenly when made well. Also try *baklawa*, a many-layered flaky pastry stuffed with nuts and honey; an alternative is *atayeef*, a deep-fried pastry with sweet or cheese filling, served principally during Ramadan. If you want something less sweet, *mahallabiyah* is a smooth pudding of rice and milk garnished with nuts.

EUROPEAN CUISINE

In tourist hotels, local cuisine is too often banished from the menu almost entirely and its place taken by 'international' cuisine (although only the best hotels employ foreign chefs). Depending on various factors, therefore, this cuisine can be bland or undistinguished, or occasionally sublime. Both in and outside the hotels, you will find a wide variety of cosmopolitan cuisine – Chinese, Indian, Japanese, Italian and French (the latter occasionally pretentious and over-priced). (See also recommended restaurants on pp.73–80.)

BEVERAGES

Moslems are forbidden to partake of alcohol. Though many Egyptians enjoy a **beer**, the religious prohibition of alcohol means that **soft drinks** are very popular, and found everywhere. Many known, western-style soft drinks are bottled under licence in Egypt, including low-calorie versions.

The good news is that you don't have to worry about the **water**. Good, safe water from local wells is bottled under licence by French mineral water companies. **Fruit juices** are usually available, sometimes freshly-squeezed. Be sure to try the speciality called *karkadeh*, a deep-red infusion of hibiscus petals with an agreeable flavour, served to you slightly sweetened. It's delicious cold

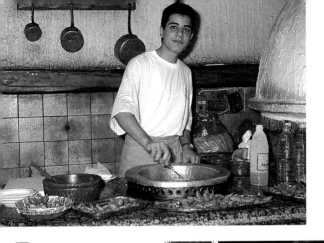

*F*orget *moderation; traditional Egyptian cuisine is colourful, copious and tasty.*

at breakfast time, but can be a bracing pick-me-up served hot as well. In Upper Egypt, where the plant grows, it is served frequently. Sugar-cane juice is also cheap and flavoursome.

Egyptian vineyards in the Delta have been cultivated for centuries. All hotel restaurants serve **wine**, though the selection may be limited (and service is suspended on Moslem religious holidays). The price of a bottle of wine in a hotel restaurant is about three times the shop price. Buy a bottle and have the steward mark it with your room number so that if you don't finish it at one meal, you can still enjoy it at the next. Of the various reds, Omar Khayyam and Château **113** (or Kasr) Gianaclis are fairly dry, with a good deal of tannin. Pharaons has less taste and is slightly more dry. White wines – Nefertiti, Cleopatra, Gianaclis Villages – are often better than red, but must be chilled. If you prefer rosé, ask for Rubis d'Egypte. Local wine is definitely an acquired taste, but imported table wine, when available, can increase the cost of your meal by more than twice.

Imported brands of **beer** are served in hotels and restaurants, always relatively expensive. The local beer is a light pleasant lager called Stella. Some may prefer the upmarket version Stella Export, which comes at a higher price.

Local **spirits** are made from either grapes or dates. *Zibib*, an Egyptian, aniseed-flavoured *arak* (like *ouzo* or *pastis*), is made from either grape brandy or date brandy. Many visitors find the grape variety preferable. Locally made vodka is good. Imported spirits take a prominent place in high-class hotel and restaurant bars, and are expensive.

Tea and Turkish Coffee

Coffee can be a problem in Egypt. French or American-style is not very good; espresso may be available, if not, opt for instant. The best solution is **Turkish coffee** – served on the slightest pretext. An Egyptian host who didn't serve coffee, even on a short visit, would be viewed as a national disgrace. Most foreigners come to prefer Turkish coffee if its brewed *mazbut* (with a medium quantity of sugar). If it tastes too bitter order it *ziyada* (with lots of sugar). *Saadeh* is with no sugar. *Arrihah* means your tiny cup will appear with only a slight pinch of sugar. In practice, you can often never be sure just how the coffee will come, for one coffee-maker's *arrihah* is another's *mazbut*.

Tea (*shay*) is popular with Egyptians and tourists alike. As a refresher in local coffee houses, it comes with sprigs of mint – stir a few in your glass, Egyptians swear it helps digestion and gives extra energy.

See the cover of this guide for useful restaurant phrases.

BLUEPRINT
for a
Perfect Trip

An A-Z Summary of Practical Information and Facts

Included after some headings is the appropriate transcription of spoken Arabic, plus a number of phrases that should be useful when seeking assistance. Beware that ongoing modernization of Egypt's communications system means that telephone numbers are subject to constant change.

A

ACCOMMODATION (see also CAMPING on p.119, NILE CRUISES on p.130, YOUTH HOSTELS on p.141 and RECOMMENDED HOTELS on pp.66-72)

Since group tour operators usually have priority in room allotment, your best guarantee of reserved accommodation is if a travel agent makes the arrangements. If you're travelling alone, make reservations well in advance and even then come armed with written confirmations – overbooking, for hotels and cruises alike, is a constant problem. For cruises in particular, a group-tour is your best bet.

Competition for rooms is most intense during the peak season of December to April. Alexandria and Mediterranean resorts are busiest in the summer months and almost deserted from November to April.

As well as a resurgence in luxury hotels, more moderately priced hotels have opened in Cairo, Luxor and at Red Sea and Sinai resorts.

Hotel rates are usually quoted in US dollars and bills can be settled by credit card, foreign currency or with Egyptian pounds. For the latter, you must have the bank's foreign-exchange receipt.

AIRPORTS

Cairo Airport has four terminals: three international and one domestic. The international terminals have a café, restaurant, bar, banks (see MONEY MATTERS on p.129) and duty-free and souvenir shops. You will need to change some money into Egyptian currency in small denominations for porter's tips and taxis. Visas are available if you neglected to get them at home – but don't complain about the delay (see also CUSTOMS AND ENTRY FORMALITIES on p.121).

Keep your camera in its bag, photography is forbidden at airports. The Egyptian Tourism Authority, near the exit of the arrivals hall, is there to help, including last-minute accommodation problems.

Make sure you have a return flight booked before you leave home and follow regulations for reconfirmation of ongoing or return reservations once you reach Egypt. Overbooking is a frequent problem and the best protection is prompt reconfirmation and early check-in.

Airport Transfers. Normal taxis, Misr Travel cars and air-conditioned buses operate between Cairo Airport and downtown hotels. In the occasional scramble for cars, it's accepted practice in Egypt to share a cab. On the day of your departure, allow plenty of time – at least two hours – both for Cairo's traffic snarls and airport bedlam.

Airports at Alexandria, Luxor, Aswân, Abu Simbel, Hurghada and Sharm El-Sheikh have hotel transfers available both by taxi and bus.

ANTIQUITIES

It is quite simply illegal to take out of the country any Egyptian antiquities, however 'honestly' acquired.

B

BAKSHEESH

The time-honoured Middle Eastern custom of informal tipping for services rendered has expanded in direct proportion to the phenomenal growth of the tourist industry. It only becomes tiresome where tourists gather *en masse* – at pyramids, museums, temples, bazaars. **117**

Seasoned travellers suspect it is the exotic flavour of the word that makes it seem more prevalent in Egypt than in Manhattan, Montmartre or the Piazza San Marco.

Tour-group leaders usually organize *baksheesh* for guides around the monuments and museums, but have some 50-piastre or one-Egyptian-pound notes available anyway (for when you're on your own), to give to the guardian that shows you an off-limits tomb in the Valley of the Kings, or a hidden treasure behind a closed door in the mosque. It is often their only source of income. All foreign currency is welcome, but single dollar-bills work wonders far beyond their face value.

BICYCLE HIRE (*igár bisiklét*)

Bikes can be rented in Luxor on both sides of the Nile, and are a leisurely way of touring the temples and tombs. Rates are low, with the usual bargaining. You can also rent bikes at many of the Red Sea and Sinai resort hotels.

What's the charge per day?   **bekám fil yom**

BOAT SERVICES

The romantic *feluccas* which ply the Nile waters are practical as well as picturesque. They will give you a more flexible timetable for your visits from Luxor to the Valley of the Kings or from Aswân to the river islands. You can arrange to hire a boat and helmsman in any Nile town or village, or at many of Cairo's riverfront hotels. If you're on a tight budget, save your *felucca* cruise for Luxor and Aswân, as rates in Cairo can be high if you are not sharing with a group. Fix the price and itinerary, especially if there's a return trip, before boarding. The local tourist office can advise you on appropriate – and approximate – prices.

The Nile Bus motorized ferry plies between Old Cairo (south) and the Television Building in the north.

For lunch or dinner on the river, see RESTAURANTS on p.136 and **118** for longer excursions see NILE CRUISES. on p.130.

CAMPING (*mo'askar*)

Camping facilities are improving in the Nile Valley, the Oases and at the Mediterranean, Red Sea and Sinai resorts. The tourist information office (see p.139) has details of sites and amenities.

CAR HIRE

With the possible exception of relatively uncomplicated resort areas like Sharm El-Sheikh in the Sinai and Hurghada on the Red Sea, it is usually too much of a hassle to drive your own rented car in Egypt. Local and international rental companies provide chauffeur-driven cars for longer tours, best reserved in advance as part of your travel package. Rental is by credit card or advance cash payment. Otherwise it's cheaper and simpler to stick to taxis.

CHILDREN'S EGYPT

If you keep the sightseeing to small doses, Egypt can be marvellous fun for youngsters, but the climate may be tough on the under-10s. Ancient monuments become much more enjoyable when visited on the back of a camel or mule. In Cairo, visit a papyrus factory and show them how hieroglyphs are painted. On the way to the pyramids at Gîza, they can see the wildlife of Egypt and the Sudan at the Zoological Gardens across the University (El Gamaa) Bridge. Promise them a mummy or two and they'll even go to the Egyptian Museum.

In Luxor and Aswân, half the fun comes with a trip in a horse-drawn carriage (*calèche*) or tall-sailed *felucca*. The alabaster carvers near the Theban Necropolis, the botanical gardens and Philae Temples on Aswân's islands, and the Aswân High Dam itself are all good places to take children.

It's a good idea to include at least one hotel with a swimming pool in your accommodation, or a visit to a Red Sea, Sinai or Mediterranean resort. Hotels can help you find a babysitter. **119**

CLIMATE

October and November are the most comfortable months to visit Egypt. April and May are also cool and pleasant, but more unpredictable. Mid-winter weather can be quite nippy, although the constant dryness of the air and almost total absence of rain (except in Alexandria and along the northern coast) give Egypt a perfectly healthy climate for the time of year.

Like the major hotels, Nile cruise boats, tour buses and trains are air-conditioned, so a visit to Egypt in summer is perfectly feasible if you plan your sightseeing early or late in the day, and take precautions against excessive sun and dryness. Cairo and the Nile Delta are more humid than Luxor and Aswân, and the resorts of the Mediterranean and the Red Sea benefit, of course, from sea breezes.

The chart below shows average monthly temperatures in Cairo and Alexandria:

		J	F	M	A	M	J	J	A	S	O	N	D
Cairo	°C	14	15	18	21	23	27	29	28	26	24	20	15
	°F	57	59	64	70	76	81	84	82	79	75	68	59
Alexandria	°C	14	15	16	19	22	24	26	27	25	23	20	16
	°F	57	59	61	66	72	75	79	81	77	76	68	61

CLOTHING

Egypt's climate demands the coolest possible cotton clothing for a visit during the hottest months from May to September, plus a broad-brimmed hat and sunglasses. Since Egyptian cotton is of superb quality, you may want to buy some lighter clothing once you arrive.

In winter (November to March) it can be surprisingly chilly at night, so take warm pullovers or a wrap. Warm clothing is necessary for evenings in the desert any time of year. Remember some first-class dining-rooms or restaurants require men to wear a jacket.

When visiting mosques, shorts are taboo for men and women alike – women should wear modest, longish dresses with sleeves, while men should wear trousers and sports shirt. In town, wear flat **120** shoes, moccasins or sandals that are easy to kick off at the entrance to a mosque. High heels are a mistake anywhere. Comfortable walking shoes are essential both for the sand and rough stone terrain of archaeological sites – as well as for the city centre, where roadworks are constantly in progress. Take more sturdy shoes – and very warm clothing – if you're planning a trip to Mount Sinai.

COMPLAINTS

If you really feel you have been cheated or misled, raise the matter first with the manager or proprietor of the establishment in question – preferably with a smile. Egyptians are generally gentle, easy-going people. Angry glares and shouting will get you nowhere. If you still do not get satisfaction, take the problem to the highly co-operative tourism authorities or, as a last resort, the Tourist Police (see TOURIST INFORMATION OFFICES on p.139 and POLICE on p.133).

CRIME

Egyptians are generally law-abiding people, but petty theft and pickpocketing do occur. Without undue paranoia, take usual precautions: watch your wallet or purse in crowded bazaars and on trains and buses, lock your luggage before handing it over to railway or airline porters, and don't leave valuables on display in your hotel room. If you are robbed, contact the Tourist Police (see POLICE on p.133).

CUSTOMS and ENTRY FORMALITIES

Everyone entering Egypt must register with the Interior Ministry at the 'Mugamaa' in Tahrir Square, Cairo, or similar immigration offices in Luxor or Alexandria, within seven days of arrival. This may be done by the hotel, tour agent, host or individually, but it must be done. Late registration may entail a fine and a bureaucratic row.

Visitors to Egypt need a valid passport and either a transit visa for a stay not exceeding seven days or a tourist visa for a period of one month (renewable for up to six months). Both are available from Egyptian consulates abroad or from passport authorities at the point of entry (for those who failed to get them back home).

When departing you may change Egyptian money back into foreign currency provided you have kept appropriate exchange receipts. **121**

The following items can be taken into Egypt duty-free and back into your own country:

Into:	Cigarettes		Cigars		Tobacco	Spirits		Wine
Egypt	200	or	25	or	200 g	1 l	or	1 l
Australia	250	or	250	or	250 g	1 l	or	1 l
Canada	200	and	50	and	1,000 g	1.1 l	or	1.1 l
Eire	200	or	50	or	250 g	1 l	and	2 l
N Zealand	200	or	50	or	250 g	1 l	and	4.5 l
S Africa	400	and	50	and	250 g	1 l	and	2 l
UK	200	or	50	or	250 g	1 l	and	2 l
USA	200	and	100	and	*	1 l	or	1 l
* a reasonable quantity								

Currency restrictions: Not more than LE 100 can be imported or exported, but there is no restriction on the amount of foreign currency you may bring into or take out of Egypt, provided it is declared to customs on arrival. The law requires visitors to list all funds in their possession on an official currency declaration form. Demand the form if it is not offered and have it stamped at customs: it must be shown with currency exchange receipts on leaving the country. It is very important to have the form available and in order, as customs officials may confiscate currency not entered on the form.

D

DISABLED TRAVELLERS
Along the Nile Valley, the desert terrain surrounding most of the ancient monuments does not make it easy for travellers to get around in a wheelchair. ETAMS Tours, the Egyptian Company for Tourism and Medical Services, 99 Ramses Street, Cairo, tel. 754 721, organizes special bus and taxi tours for the disabled. Facilities at the modern hotels of the Mediterranean, Red Sea and Sinai resorts are as good as anywhere in the world.

DRIVING

Unless you already know the country well or your spirit of adventure defies hazards rarely encountered on even the most hair-raising roads of Europe, we would recommend against bringing your own car to Egypt. If you do, you will need:

• International driving licence

• Car registration papers

• *Carnet de passage*

The above documents exempt you from paying tax or having to pass an Egyptian driver's test. You will have to purchase third-party liability insurance in Egypt.

Driving conditions. The Egyptian authorities have not made it illegal for foreigners to drive inside the Cairo city-limits. This is an oversight. Only local residents have even the remotest idea of how to handle traffic jams on the main roads, side-streets, downtown squares and roundabouts. Combat for parking makes the average Arab-Israeli war seem like croquet. Outside the capital, roads are serviceable but beset by pharaonic farm-vehicles, pedestrians and cattle quite properly claiming right of way. Road signs are rare and esoteric. For further information on driving laws and assistance or advice with any automobile issue, contact: Automobile Club of Egypt, 10 Sharia Kasr El Nil, Cairo, tel. 574 3355.

Distance

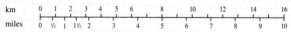

Fluid measures

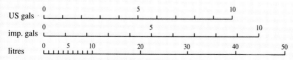

driving licence	**rókhsit alkiyáda**
insurance policy	**bolísit alta'mín**
Are we on the right road for …?	**húa da at-tarík li …**
Fill the tank, please.	**imlá il tank min fádlak**
normal/super	**ádi/súbar**
Check the oil/tires/battery, please.	**min fádlak shoof al zayt/al ágal/al batMaría**
I've broken down.	**arabíyiti itattálit**
There's been an accident.	**fih hádsa**

E

ELECTRIC CURRENT

Practically all of Egypt has 220-volt, 50-cycle electric current. Sockets are of the European type with two cylindrical prongs. The current, however, may not be constantly at full voltage strength. In case of power failure in your hotel room, you will usually find a candle in the bedside table or bathroom.

EMBASSIES and CONSULATES *(safára; konsolía)*

Australia: Embassy, Cairo Plaza, Corniche El-Nil; tel. 777 900.

Canada: Embassy, 8 Mohammed Fahmy El-Sayed Street, Garden City, Cairo; tel. 354 3110.

Eire: Embassy, 3 Abou El-Feda St, Zamalek; tel. 340 8264.

UK: Embassy, 7 Ahmed Ragheb Street, Garden City, Cairo; tel. 354 0852.

Consulate, 3 Mena Street, Roushdy, Alexandria; tel. 546 7001.

USA: Embassy, 8 Kamel El-Dih Street, Garden City, Cairo; tel. 357 2462.

Consulate, 110 Avenue El-Horreya, Alexandria; tel. 481 1911.

EMERGENCIES

If your hotel receptionist or a Tourist Police officer is not at hand to help, you can telephone these numbers:

Police	**122**
Ambulance	**121**
Fire service	**125**

All hospitals have an ambulance service, but remember in Cairo that traffic will cause delays.

ETIQUETTE

There is little formality to Egyptian manners. The people are warm and affable and the first part of a greeting is a natural smile, often accompanied by a raised right hand, before a firm handshake. Nevertheless, Egyptians do not indulge in or appreciate public displays of intimacy. In a restaurant, blowing your nose is positively offensive.

It is customary to accompany business or commercial dealings with a cup of coffee or tea and indeed it is considered impolite to refuse it – accepting a drink implies no obligation to close a deal.

Egyptians welcome non-Moslems to mosques, though prayer times and the Friday sabbath should be avoided. Dress modestly and remove your shoes before entering. Be discreet when photographing and even outside, ask permission before taking someone's picture.

GETTING TO EGYPT
BY AIR
Scheduled flights

Scheduled services operate daily from London's Heathrow and Gatwick airports. Irish and provincial flights make the connection in London for the 4-hour non-stop flight to Cairo. Daily direct flights link New York and Cairo, with connecting services available from major cities in the United States and Canada.

Charter Flights and Package Tours

From the UK: There is a wide range of package tours to Egypt, the more expensive ones including a Nile cruise with accommodation, meals and sightseeing. Some charter flights and cheaper options are available to Luxor and Sharm El-Sheikh, as well as Cairo, but conditions constantly change, so check details with your travel agent.

From North America: There are currently dozens of GITs (Group Inclusive Tours) available to Egypt for periods of 7 to 22 days, with Cairo as the starting point. Tour features include return flights, hotel accommodation, some or all meals, transfers and porterage, sightseeing, the services of an English-speaking guide, taxes, and all service charges. Optional features include a Nile river cruise, lasting from 4 to 8 days, or an air tour to Abu Simbel.

BY LAND AND SEA

You can take the train or drive your car to Venice or Athens to catch the ship to Alexandria. Few of them are true car ferries (though most carry cars), so it's particularly important to check sailing schedules and prices with your travel agent before leaving home, as well as booking your passage at least two weeks in advance.

Some Mediterranean cruises call at Alexandria or Port Said, giving passengers the opportunity for a trip to Cairo and the pyramids.

GUIDES (dalíl)

Only guides licensed by the Ministry of Tourism in Egypt are permitted into historical sites. You can arrange for a licensed guide through any hotel or travel agency. Make sure beforehand that everyone understands your personal requirements – fluency in foreign languages and real knowledge of history and antiquities – and what you're prepared to pay. Beyond any cultural expertise, a guide is particularly useful, for instance, in helping you find your way around the tombs at the Valley of the Kings or the mosques of Islamic Cairo.

We'd like an English-speaking guide.	**aízin dalíl bil lógha el-inglízi**
I need an English interpreter.	**aíz mutérgim inglízi**

LANGUAGE (see also NUMBERS on p.142)

Arabic is the predominant and official language of Egypt, and indeed Egyptian Arabic is widely regarded as the 'standard' for the Arabic-speaking world, which covers dozens of Arabic dialects. Staff in large hotels usually speak some English, French and, increasingly, German, with some Italian along the Mediterranean. On the street, people speak a few words of English or French.

General expressions are listed on the front of this guide, and some 'restaurant' Arabic on the back. The Berlitz ARABIC PHRASE BOOK AND DICTIONARY covers most situations you're likely to encounter.

Good morning.	**sabáhil khayr**
Good evening.	**masá'il khayr**
Goodbye.	**ma'assaláma**
Thank you.	**shúkran/muttshékkir**
Do you speak English?	**bititkállim inglízi**

LAUNDRY and DRY-CLEANING

(ghaséel; tandéef bil bokhár)

Your hotel can arrange for good laundry and dry-cleaning services, usually same day at no extra charge if handed in at breakfast time.

When will it be ready?	**ímta takún gáhiza**
I need it … today/tomorrow	**aízha … ennahárda/bókra**

LOST PROPERTY

Save time and energy by appealing only to senior staff at hotels or museums. For items lost on the train, talk to the conductor or, when you get off, the station-master. If you've left something in a taxi taken from or to your hotel, the Tourist Police may be able to help, as records are kept of taxi movements to major tourist destinations. **127**

MEDICAL CARE (See also EMERGENCIES on p.125)

Ask your insurance company before leaving home if your policy covers medical treatment in Egypt. Combined change of climate and diet can cause intestinal upsets for which your doctor probably has a simple preventive or curative remedy. Good bottled mineral water is easily available all over Egypt. Drink it both for your stomach's sake and against dehydration – even if you don't feel particularly thirsty.

The sun is a constant threat. Wear a hat and sunglasses and use a protective lotion for both before and after exposure. Bring insect repellant for use against flies and mosquitoes, or buy one of the sprays available in Egypt; local brands tend to be more effective. Malaria is not generally a problem in the main tourist areas, but this volatile disease does occasionally crop up in the Nile Delta or in the remote south, so check with a qualified doctor.

The Nile waters are inhabited by a dangerous flat worm parasite called bilharzia. Don't swim in the river or walk barefoot near it.

Chemists'/Druggists' (*agzakhána*). Look out for the shop sign of a blue crescent with a green cross or serpent within it. Many stay open long hours, even 24 hours a day. Local medicines may not have the same name as back home, so check first with a hotel doctor. Here are some of Cairo's better pharmacies, catering both to Egyptians and foreign visitors:

Zarif, Talaat Harb Square; tel. 393 6347.

Esaaf (24-hour service), 37 July 26th Street; tel. 743 369.

Hospital: Anglo-American Hospital (behind Cairo Tower), Zohorreya, Zamalek; tel. 340 6162.

Vaccinations. Check with your travel agency whether the region from where you are travelling to Egypt obliges you to have an international vaccination certificate.

128 I need a doctor/dentist.   **aíz doktór/doktór asnáan**

MONEY MATTERS (For Currency Restrictions, see Customs and Entry Formalities on p. 121)

Currency: The Egyptian *pound* (LE) is divided into 100 *piastres* (pt). You may see prices written several ways: LE 1.50, LE 1.500 or 150 pt – which all mean the same amount of money, one and a half pounds. Banknotes range from 25 and 50 pt to LE 1, 5, 10, 20, 50 and 100. Coins come in 5, 10, 20 and 25 pt pieces.

Banking hours: 8.30am to 2pm Sunday to Thursday. All city banks are closed on Friday and Saturday, but banking desks at the airports, in the larger hotels and aboard most cruise boats have special hours for the convenience of tourists.

Changing money: It is illegal to exchange foreign currency except at a bank or other authorized establishments. Be sure to obtain official receipts; these are necessary to justify your expenditures and to prove you have not changed money on the black market. Also, reconvert Egyptian money to foreign currency before you leave.

There are bank desks before the check-in counters and passport control at Cairo Airport.

Credit Cards and Traveller's Cheques: More and more establishments accept and even prefer credit cards. Always check the 'Total' amount you're signing for is filled in below the 'Tips' entry, and not above it. Traveller's cheques are best cashed at banks or in hotels.

NEWSPAPERS and MAGAZINES

International periodicals come in a day or two late. It is worth looking at the English-language *Egyptian Gazette* or its French-language equivalent for the official government view of national and world events. *Cairo Today* is an attractive, lively monthly magazine which is particularly informative on trends in shopping and local gastronomy around the country.

NILE CRUISES

If at all possible, include a Nile cruise as part of your stay in Egypt. Luxury and other more modest but comfortable cruise boats are run by hotel chains and major travel companies. Since demand often exceeds that of land-based hotel rooms, reservations are best made back home through your travel agency well in advance. However, last-minute space is sometimes available on the spot through local agents. The most common itinerary starts out from Luxor or Aswân, cruising between the two points for 5 to 8 days and stopping at major temples and sights on the way. There are also longer trips from and to Cairo, usually at the beginning and end of the season.

The Egyptian Hotel Association lists over 160 vessels cruising the river between Cairo and Aswân. We list below a few of the leading cruise organizers, most with fleets ranging from modest 2-star riverboats to luxury 5-star cruise-ships and varying in price according to overall package. All companies below are in Cairo/the Cairo area.

Abercrombie & Kent, 5A Bustan Street; tel. 765 432, fax 757 486.

Cataract Nile Cruises, 26 Adan Street, Mohandessin; tel. 361 6231, fax 360 0864.

Club Méditerranée, 48 Mossadak Street, Dokki; tel. 361 4441, fax 360 1912.

Hilton Cruises, Nile Hilton Hotel, Tahrir Square; tel. 578 0666, fax 574 0880.

Nile Crocodile, 41 Abdel Khalek Sarwad Street; tel. 391 4554, fax 392 8153.

Oberoi Cruises, Mena House Hotel, Gîza; tel. 383 1225, 383 3222, fax 383 1227.

Presidential Nile Cruises, 13 Maraashli Street, Zamalek; tel. 340 0517, fax 340 5272.

Sheraton Nile Cruises, 4 Ahmed Naguib Street, Garden City; tel. 355 6664, fax 355 8100.

Sofitel Nile Scarabee, Cornish El Nil, Garden City; tel. 355 4481.

OPENING HOURS

Shops. In Cairo, shops open from 10am to 7pm in winter, and 10am to 8pm in summer, closing one hour later on Monday and Thursday all year round. The afternoon siesta is sacred. Government shops close between 2 and 5pm every day. Although there is no consistency in closing for private shops, generally the 2 to 5pm time slot is observed. Cairo's Khan El-Khalili bazaar closes at 8pm. Shops have no fixed closing hours during Ramadan. A few close on Friday, most on Sunday, and some stay open until the early hours of the morning.

Museums (in Cairo): Most are open every day of the week:

major establishments: from 9am to 5pm, with a break from 11.30am to 1.30pm on Friday.

smaller museums: in winter, daily 9am to 1pm, on Friday to 11.30am. In summer, some Cairo museums close at 2.30pm.

PHOTOGRAPHY

When buying film, remember that the light in Egypt is dazzling, particularly around the sand and limestone of the ancient monuments.

Almost none of Egypt's important museums allows visitors to take photographs, and you will often be asked to leave your camera at the door. Photography is also forbidden in most ancient tombs. Some places do permit photography for a fee, which can be quite expensive for video cameras. The bans should be respected as automatic flashes pose a great threat to the fragile colour of the pharaonic monuments.

Do not take pictures of bridges, public buildings, airports, or other 'strategically sensitive' places, and ask permission before taking photographs of people or inside mosques or churches.

May I take a picture?   **múmkin ákhod súra**

PLANNING YOUR BUDGET

Here's a list of average prices in Egyptian *pounds* (LE), *piastres* (pt) and US dollars. Bear in mind inflation and tipping or *baksheesh*.

Airport. Porter 50 pt per bag. Hire of baggage trolley LE 1. Taxi to centre of Cairo LE 27, by limousine LE 18.

Boat services. *Felucca* (per hour for entire boat) LE 20-25 in Cairo, LE 20-25 in Aswân and Luxor. Nile bus LE 1.50 to Old Cairo, LE 2 to Nile Barrages.

Car hire (with unlimited mileage). *Fiat 128* $50-56 per day; *Fiat Nova Regat* (air-conditioned) $72-83 per day; *Peugeot 505* (air-conditioned estate) $86-117 per day. Add $1.25 personal insurance per day and 5% local tax.

Cigarettes. Egyptian filters LE 2 for 20, foreign brands LE 3.50.

Entertainment. Cinemas LE 2.50-5.50, discotheque LE 15-20, nightclub (including dinner but not drinks) LE 40-60.

Guides. LE 10-15 per hour depending on language and place.

Hotels (double room with bath per night). Luxury class $120-160, first class $90-120, second class $40-75, third class $25-35. Add 12% service, 14% municipal tax. Breakfast LE 12-18 per day.

Food and drink. Continental breakfast LE 8-20, lunch/dinner in fairly good establishment LE 10-40, *ful* and *taamia* LE 1.50, bottled soft drinks LE 1, coffee LE 1-1.50, local beer LE 4, imported beer (small can) LE 10, Egyptian wine (bottle) LE 18, cocktail LE 33, mineral water LE 2.50 per litre.

Museums. LE 5-10.

Nile Cruises. 4 to 7 nights $344-800 per person double occupancy.

Transport. *Train* Cairo to Alexandria LE 25-42, special tourist train (overnight sleeper) Cairo to Luxor or Aswân, LE 216 per person, including meals. *Air* Cairo to: Luxor $75, Aswân $103, Abu Simbel $164, Hurghada $80, Sharm El-Sheikh $85, Alexandria $42.

POLICE (*bolís*) (see also EMERGENCIES on p.125.)

Cairo and Alexandria policemen wear white uniforms in summer, black in winter. In the provinces you'll see officers in khaki. Tourist Police officers, some of whom speak English or other languages, have normal uniforms with an added green and white armband and the words 'Tourist Police' in English and Arabic. They are a discreet presence around the main tourist sites and bazaars, and are contactable through any official tourist information office (see p.139).

In Cairo, the Tourist Police Public Service telephone number is **126**. Their headquarters is at 5 Adly Street, tel. 247 2584. Telephone numbers for police elsewhere are: Alexandria: 863 804; Luxor: 82120; Aswân: 23163.

POST OFFICE

The postal service in Egypt is unpredictable. Postcards are taken less seriously than letters and may be delayed. For important messages stick to fax, telex or the telephone. If you expect to receive mail, have it sent to a hotel address rather than the less reliable poste restante.

Public post boxes come in such a bewildering variety of colours and markings according to their express, air mail or ordinary mail function that you are better off relying on your hotel facilities.

Hours: Cairo's main post office in Ataba Square is open from 8am to 3pm and 5 to 7pm daily except Friday. Other offices are open from 8.30am to 3pm daily except Friday.

PUBLIC HOLIDAYS

Moslem religious holidays are also national holidays in Egypt. If a Moslem feast lasts more than a day, shops and offices will close on the first day and open with shorter hours on the others. During Ramadan, when Moslems fast during daylight hours, shorter working hours apply in almost all offices, and shops are open very late into the night. Coptic (Christian) holidays are not treated as national holidays, though Coptic-run shops and businesses may close. The Coptic calendar is different from the western Christian Gregorian calendar: Coptic Christmas is celebrated, for instance, on 7 January. **133**

Secular Holidays:

January 1	*New Year's Day* (banks only)
First Monday after Coptic Easter (National Spring Festival)	*Sham En Nessim*
April 25	*Sinai Day*
May 1	*Labour Day*
July 23	*Revolution Day*
October 6	*Armed Forces Day*

Religious Holidays. As the Islamic calendar is lunar, its religious holidays vary greatly from year to year on the standard Gregorian calendar. In Islamic reckoning, a day starts at sundown. If you're told a particular day is a religious holiday, expect the celebrations to begin at sundown the day before. Businesses close on the eve of a holiday and restaurants which stay open may not serve alcohol.

PUBLIC TRANSPORT

Buses in Cairo are so crammed as to be impractical. For trips from the centre of town to the Coptic sights of Old Cairo, you may try the Nile Bus which runs from the jetty opposite the Television Building upriver to the terminus at Old Cairo. (The Coptic quarter is a 5-minute walk from the terminus.) The 40-minute journey offers welcome respite from the traffic noise, making about five stops *en route*.

The downtown Cairo metro **underground train** service is expanding. Fast, clean and efficient, it is a useful way of getting from Tahrir Square to Mar Girgis Station for the Coptic Museum and Old Cairo.

Frequent **day trains** run between Cairo and Alexandria. Overnight trains from Cairo Station have air-conditioned sleeping and restaurant cars for the Nile Valley route via Minia and Assiut to Luxor and Aswân, and back. First class is comfortable, second class adequate; advance reservations are advisable. There is also a special and faster luxury tourist train between Cairo and Aswân, with an all-in price (not cheap) including meals and sleeping-berths.

Domestic Air Routes: for EgyptAir's domestic flights, advance bookings and reconfirmation are essential. Not all services are daily, so plan itineraries carefully. Flights operate between Cairo, Luxor, Aswân, Abu Simbel, New Valley (for the Western Desert Oases), Alexandria and Mersa Matruh for the Mediterranean, Hurghada for the Red Sea and, with the Air Sinai subsidiary, Sharm El-Sheikh.

Chauffeur Service: limousines provide a comfortable and reliable means of transport in Cairo. Be sure to agree on the fare beforehand.

Horse-cabs: romantic horse-drawn carriages – commonly known as *calèches* – in Luxor, Aswân and throughout the Nile Valley are regulated by an official price list. Consult the list in the Tourist Office (see p.139) before taking a ride – you may have to haggle for a price in any case. There are even a few still in Cairo, if you can bear the traffic fumes!

Where's the bus for ...? **fayn al otobís illi ráyih ...**

R

RADIO and TV (*rádyo; tilivísyon*)

If you don't have your own portable shortwave radio for the BBC or Voice of America (check wavelengths before leaving home), Egypt's multilingual radio station broadcasts from 7am to midnight daily. In the course of the day, it has news and feature programmes in English, French, Italian, German, Greek and Armenian. For the schedule, consult the Cairo daily newspapers, *The Egyptian Gazette*, *Le Journal d'Egypte* or *Le Progrès Egyptien*.

Egyptian state television broadcasts on three channels. Channel 2 has daily news in English and French. Major hotels also carry CNN from the US, the BBC World Service and other British satellite TV, French-language TV5, RAI from Italy, and German satellite TV.

RELIGION

Egypt is predominantly Moslem, with a sizeable Christian (mainly Coptic) minority. Catholic and Protestant services are held in Cairo, Luxor and Aswân. In Cairo and Alexandria, there are synagogues (Israeli Embassy, tel. 361 0545, can provide details). For a complete listing of Sunday services, consult either the Saturday issue of *The Egyptian Gazette*, called *The Egyptian Mail*, or the magazine *Cairo Today*, which comes out monthly.

RESTAURANTS (see also EATING OUT on p.109 and the list of RECOMMENDED RESTAURANTS on pp.73-80)

You can dine while floating down the Nile on boats serving Egyptian and European cuisine, or lunch and dinner with musical entertainment. Boats which are not described as 'cruising restaurant' remain tied to their mooring.

CAIRO

Alf Laila Cruising Restaurant, Corniche El-Nil, Garden City; tel. 354 0417.

Golden Pharaoh Cruising Restaurant, 31 Corniche El-Nil, Gîza; tel. 570 1000.

Nile Pharaoh, 31 Corniche El-Nil, Gîza; tel. 570 1000.

Saladin, El-Nil Street, Gîza (front of Foreign Ministry); tel. 731 370.

Scarabee Cruising Restaurant, Corniche El-Nil (in front of Shepheard's Hotel); tel. 355 4481.

Sunset, 33 El-Nil, Gîza (behind French Embassy); tel. 729 261.

LUXOR

Hotel cruise-boats serve dinner sailing past the sights of Luxor and Karnak, or lunch on a cruise north to the Temple of Denderah.

Le Lotus, Novotel Evasion, Khaled Ibn El-Walid Street; tel. 580 925.

M.S.Africa, Mövenpick Jolie Ville, Crocodile Island; tel. 374 855.

Meri Ra, Sheraton Luxor, El-Awameya Road; tel. 374 544.

TAXIS

Some taxis have meters, but drivers will not always run them, giving the (often valid) excuse that the machine is out of order. To avoid unpleasant surprises, agree fares in advance, with tip included. It is useful to be able to tell the driver your destination in Arabic, as many speak nothing else (ask your hotel to write the address in Arabic).

Taxi ranks are found near the larger hotels, tourist attractions, and at the airport, but normal procedure is to stop a taxi in the street. Note that a Tourist Police officer is on duty near each rank, laboriously recording each cab's number, time of departure and destination.

In most towns an official table of rates is established by the authorities, but it is sometimes difficult to discover what the correct fare should be. Often it is best to strike a bargain with the driver until you can get a list of fares from the tourist information office (see p.139).

Shared Taxis: every city and town in Egypt has shared taxis for intercity travel. Fares are fixed, cheap, and the cars move out once full. The majority are seven-seat Peugeots or Mercedes. Fare supervision is strict and very rarely will the driver ask for more. Tips are not expected. Generally they will not operate, on a lengthy run, after 8pm. Cairo has several ranks – one for Alexandria, one for the canal cities etc. These are located close to the main railway or bus station for a particular destination as the taxis absorb the surplus traffic. Fares are very slightly more than the bus, sometimes less than the train. If the overall price for all seven places is reasonable, a group of four could leave immediately by buying the remaining seats. (Don't confuse this official shared-taxi system with the increasingly prevalent sharing of an ordinary taxi around town with someone heading the same way. This practice is not strictly legal but can be very convenient.)

Taxi!	**taksi**
What's the fare to...?	**bekám li...**
Take me to...	**khódni li...**

TELEPHONE

Egypt's telephone system is undergoing extensive modernization, and service, especially in Cairo, has improved considerably. As a result, however, numbers change constantly, so check them carefully. Ask your hotel operator or dial 140 or 141 for directory information.

Public telephones are most commonly found in cigarette shops – very often just a normal desk set with a coin box attached. Shops or restaurants will let you use their telephones to make local calls if you pay in advance.

Remember that telephone calls, telex and fax messages from your hotel are charged at a much higher rate than normal, but the convenience may make it worthwhile. Using the public telephone at the post office avoids surcharges, but you may have to book an overseas call up to 24 hours in advance.

For contacting hotels in advance from back home, the following are international telephone/fax codes: Alexandria 20.3; Aswân, Abu Simbel 20.97; Cairo 20.2; Ismailiya 20.64; Luxor 20.95; The Oases 20.88; Port Said 20.66; Red Sea 20.65; Suez City, Sinai 20.62.

TIME DIFFERENCES

Egyptian time is GMT + 2. Clocks go forward an hour in summer.

Los Angeles	New York	London	Paris	**Egypt**
2am	5am	10am	11am	**noon**

TIPPING (see also BAKSHEESH on p.117)

Alhough service charge is almost always included in hotel and restaurant bills, it is customary to leave an additional tip. You are also expected to give a little extra to porters, bellboys, cinema and theatre ushers for their services. The chart below gives a few suggestions as to how much should be given.

Porter, per bag	LE 1
Maid, per week	LE 10
Waiter	10%

Table attendant	3-5%
Lavatory attendant	50 pt
Taxi driver	LE 1
Tour guide	10%
Cruise guide, per week	LE 20
Hairdresser	10%
Felucca boatman	LE 1 per passenger

TOILETS (*twalét*)

Public facilities are located in important museums and terminals, and you may use those in the larger hotels as well. If you use the facilities in a café or restaurant, it is usual to order a coffee or a bottled drink. The attendant will expect a small tip.

Toilets are usually marked with symbols of a man or a woman. Sometimes the attendant will direct you to use the 'wrong' one, but he has his reasons – more often than not to do with failed plumbing – and will stand guard to prevent embarrassment.

Where are the toilets?   **fayn al twalét**

TOURIST INFORMATION OFFICES

The Egyptian Ministry of Tourism has Information Offices in all the larger Egyptian cities, and in many foreign countries as well. They are eager to help and provide brochures, maps and detailed advice on itineraries. Once in Egypt, they can help you with information about local accommodation and practical problems.

Cairo: Ministry of Tourism, 5 Adly Street; tel. 390 3000 or 390 1835. (Other offices at Cairo Airport and at the Pyramids.)

Alexandria: Saad Zaghloul Square; tel. 482 0258.

Luxor: Tourist Market, just south of Luxor Temple; tel. 82215.

Aswân: North of old part of town, just off Corniche; tel. 23297.

Egyptian Tourist Offices abroad:

Canada: Place Bonaventure 40, Frontenac, PO Box 304, Montreal, PQ H5A 1V4; tel. (514) 861 4420.

UK: 168 Piccadilly, London, W1; tel. (071) 493 5282.

USA: 630 Fifth Avenue, New York, NY10111; tel. (212) 246 6960. Suite 608, 323 Geary Street, San Francisco, CA 94102; tel. (415) 781 7676.

WATER (máyya)

The Egyptians are fond of a local saying which decrees that if a visitor drinks even a little water from the Nile, he will return to Egypt for sure. Foreigners have a saying that he won't even leave.

Tap water in Aswân, Luxor and Cairo is channelled in from the Nile by way of a purification plant, and the authorities insist it is safe to drink. Even if it is, however, its taste is far from that of the fresh water most of us are used to, and you will probably end up drinking mineral water for most of your stay. It goes without saying, of course, that no matter how much you hope to return to Egypt, don't ever drink *directly* from the Nile.

You're safest of all with the local bottled mineral water. The most popular brand is produced as a joint venture with Vittel of France, and is called *Baraka*, which is a most appropriate Arabic word meaning 'blessing' or 'good luck'. It is perfectly acceptable to take the bottle along with you from a restaurant or hotel dining room if it is not finished at the end of your meal.

I'd like some mineral water.	**aíz máyya ma'daníyya**
fizzy (carbonated)/still	**gazzíyya/áada**
140 Is this drinking water?	**di máyya lil shurb**

WEIGHTS AND MEASURES (For fluid and distance measures see DRIVING on p.123)

Temperature

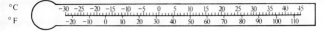

Length

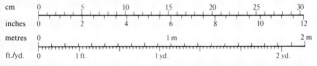

Weight

grams
ounces

YOUTH HOSTELS (*bayt shabáb*)

Hostels in Egypt's main cities offer a place to stay for a very low price, though standards of comfort vary. The best hostels are often full, and advance reservations by mail are advised. For full information contact the Egyptian Youth Hostel Association, 7 Doctor Abdel Hamid Said Street, Marrouf, Cairo; tel. 758 099. There are hostels at the following locations:

Cairo: Al Manyal Youth Hostel, 135 Abdel Aziz Al Saud Street, Manyal; tel. 840 729.

Alexandria: El-Shatbi New Youth Hotel, 23 Port Said Street, Shatbi; tel. 75459.

Aswân: Abtal El-Tahrir; tel. 2313.

NUMBERS

Listed below are the principal numbers with the corresponding Arabic figures, English phonetics and Arabic script. Unlike Arabic text, numbers are written from left to right. Some familiarity with numbers is particularly useful when checking prices while shopping.

0	·	ṣifr	صفر
1	١	**waaH**id/**waaH**dæ	واحد/واحدة
2	٢	itnain	اثنين
3	٣	tælaatæ	ثلاثة
4	٤	arba'a	أربعة
5	٥	**khæm**sæ	خمسة
6	٦	**sit**tæ	ستة
7	٧	**sæb**æ'	سبعة
8	٨	tæ**maan**yæ	ثمانية
9	٩	**tis**'æ	تسعة
10	١·	'**ash**ara	عشرة
11	١١	Hi**daa**shar	حداشر
12	١٢	it**naa**shar	اثناشر
13	١٣	tælæt**taa**shar	تلتاشر
14	١٤	arba'a**taa**shar	أربعتاشر
15	١٥	khæmæs**taa**shar	خمستاشر
16	١٦	sit**taa**shar	ستاشر
17	١٧	sæbæ'**taa**shar	سبعتاشر
18	١٨	tæmæn**taa**shar	ثمنتاشر
19	١٩	tis'æ**taa**shar	تسعتاشر
20	٢·	**ish**reen	عشرين
30	٣·	tælæ**teen**	ثلاثين
40	٤·	arba'**een**	أربعين
50	٥·	khæm**seen**	خمسين
100	١··	**mee**yæ	مية
1,000	١···	ælf	ألف

142

Index

Numbers in **bold** refer to the main entry listed.

049/604 LUD